6th Workshop on Vision and Language (VL 2017)

Valencia, Spain
4 April 2017

ISBN: 978-1-5108-3873-4

Printed from e-media with permission by:

Curran Associates, Inc.
57 Morehouse Lane
Red Hook, NY 12571

Some format issues inherent in the e-media version may also appear in this print version.

Printed by Curran Associates, Inc. (2017)

For permission requests, please contact the Association for Computational Linguistics
at the address below.

Association for Computational Linguistics
209 N. Eighth Street
Stroudsburg, Pennsylvania 18360

Phone: 1-570-476-8006
Fax: 1-570-476-0860

acl@aclweb.org

Additional copies of this publication are available from:

Curran Associates, Inc.
57 Morehouse Lane
Red Hook, NY 12571 USA
Phone: 845-758-0400
Fax: 845-758-2633
Email: curran@proceedings.com
Web: www.proceedings.com

VL 2017

The 6th Workshop on Vision and Language

Proceedings of the Workshop

April 4, 2017
Valencia, Spain

This workshop is supported by ICT COST Action IC1307, the European Network on Integrating Vision and Language (iV&L Net): Combining Computer Vision and Language Processing For Advanced Search, Retrieval, Annotation and Description of Visual Data.

Introduction

The 6th Workshop on Vision and Language 2017 (VL'17) took place in Valencia as part of EACL'17. The workshop is organised by the European Network on Integrating Vision and Language which is funded as a European COST Action. The VL workshops have the general aims: to provide a forum for reporting and discussing planned, ongoing and completed research that involves both language and vision; and to enable NLP and computer vision researchers to meet, exchange ideas, expertise and technology, and form new research partnerships.

Research involving both language and vision computing spans a variety of disciplines and applications, and goes back a number of decades. In a recent scene shift, the big data era has thrown up a multitude of tasks in which vision and language are inherently linked. The explosive growth of visual and textual data, both online and in private repositories by diverse institutions and companies, has led to urgent requirements in terms of search, processing and management of digital content. Solutions for providing access to or mining such data effectively depend on the connection between visual and textual content being made interpretable, hence on the 'semantic gap' between vision and language being bridged.

One perspective has been integrated modelling of language and vision, with approaches located at different points between the structured, cognitive modelling end of the spectrum, and the unsupervised machine learning end, with state-of-the-art results in many areas currently being produced at the latter end, in particular by deep learning approaches.

Another perspective is exploring how knowledge about language can help with predominantly visual tasks, and vice versa. Visual interpretation can be aided by text associated with images/videos and knowledge about the world learned from language. On the NLP side, images can help ground language in the physical world, allowing us to develop models for semantics. Words and pictures are often naturally linked online and in the real world, and each modality can provide reinforcing information to aid the other.

We would like to thank all the people who have contributed to the organisation and delivery of this workshop: the authors who submitted high quality papers; the programme committee for their prompt and effective reviewing; our keynote speakers; the ACL 2017 organising committee, and future readers of these proceedings for your shared interest in this exciting area of research.

April 2017,
Anja Belz, Erkut Erdem, Katerina Pastra and Krystian Mikolajczyk

Organizers:

Anya Belz, University of Brighton, UK
Erkut Erdem, Hacettepe University, Turkey
Katerina Pastra, Cognitive Systems Research Institute (CSRI), Greece
Krystian Mikolajczyk, Imperial College London, UK

Program Committee:

Raffaella Bernardi, University of Trento, Italy
Darren Cosker, University of Bath, UK
Aykut Erdem, Hacettepe University, Turkey
Jacob Goldberger, Bar Ilan University, Israel
Jordi Gonzalez, CVC UAB Barcelona, Spain
Douwe Kiela, University of Cambridge, UK
Arnau Ramisa, IRI UPC Barcelona, Spain
Josiah Wang, University of Sheffield, UK

Table of Contents

The BURCHAK corpus: a Challenge Data Set for Interactive Learning of Visually Grounded Word Meanings
Yanchao Yu, Arash Eshghi, Gregory Mills and Oliver Lemon 1

The Use of Object Labels and Spatial Prepositions as Keywords in a Web-Retrieval-Based Image Caption Generation System
Brandon Birmingham and Adrian Muscat 11

Learning to Recognize Animals by Watching Documentaries: Using Subtitles as Weak Supervision
Aparna Nurani Venkitasubramanian, Tinne Tuytelaars and Marie-Francine Moens 21

Human Evaluation of Multi-modal Neural Machine Translation: A Case-Study on E-Commerce Listing Titles
Iacer Calixto, Daniel Stein, Evgeny Matusov, Sheila Castilho and Andy Way 31

The BreakingNews Dataset
Arnau Ramisa, Fei Yan, Francesc Moreno-Noguer and Krystian Mikolajczyk 38

Automatic identification of head movements in video-recorded conversations: can words help?
Patrizia Paggio, Costanza Navarretta and Bart Jongejan 40

Multi-Modal Fashion Product Retrieval
Antonio Rubio Romano, LongLong Yu, Edgar Simo-Serra and Francesc Moreno-Noguer 43

Workshop Program

Tuesday, 4 April, 2017

9:15–9:30 ***Welcome and Opening Remarks***

9:30–10:30 *Invited Talk*
Prof. David Hogg

10:30–11:00 *The BURCHAK corpus: a Challenge Data Set for Interactive Learning of Visually Grounded Word Meanings*
Yanchao Yu, Arash Eshghi, Gregory Mills and Oliver Lemon

11:00–11:30 ***Coffee Break***

11:30–12:00 *The Use of Object Labels and Spatial Prepositions as Keywords in a Web-Retrieval-Based Image Caption Generation System*
Brandon Birmingham and Adrian Muscat

12:00–12:30 *Learning to Recognize Animals by Watching Documentaries: Using Subtitles as Weak Supervision*
Aparna Nurani Venkitasubramanian, Tinne Tuytelaars and Marie-Francine Moens

12:30–13:00 *Human Evaluation of Multi-modal Neural Machine Translation: A Case-Study on E-Commerce Listing Titles*
Iacer Calixto, Daniel Stein, Evgeny Matusov, Sheila Castilho and Andy Way

13:00–15:00 ***Lunch Break***

15:00–16:00 ***Poster Session including Quick Poster Presentations***

15:30–15:40 *The BreakingNews Dataset*
Arnau Ramisa, Fei Yan, Francesc Moreno-Noguer and Krystian Mikolajczyk

15:40–15:50 *Automatic identification of head movements in video-recorded conversations: can words help?*
Patrizia Paggio, Costanza Navarretta and Bart Jongejan

15:50–16:00 *Multi-Modal Fashion Product Retrieval*
Antonio Rubio Romano, LongLong Yu, Edgar Simo-Serra and Francesc Moreno-Noguer

16:00–16:30 ***Coffee Break***

Tuesday, 4 April, 2017 (continued)

16:30–17:30 *Invited Talk*
Prof. Mirella Lapata

The BURCHAK corpus: a Challenge Data Set for Interactive Learning of Visually Grounded Word Meanings

Yanchao Yu
Interaction Lab
Heriot-Watt University
y.yu@hw.ac.uk

Arash Eshghi
Interaction Lab
Heriot-Watt University
a.eshghi@hw.ac.uk

Gregory Mills
University of Groningen
g.j.mills@rug.nl

Oliver Lemon
Interaction Lab
Heriot-Watt University
o.lemon@hw.ac.uk

Abstract

We motivate and describe a new freely available human-human dialogue data set for interactive learning of visually grounded word meanings through ostensive definition by a tutor to a learner. The data has been collected using a novel, character-by-character variant of *the DiET chat tool* (Healey et al., 2003; Mills and Healey, submitted) with a novel task, where a Learner needs to learn invented visual attribute words (such as "burchak" for square) from a tutor. As such, the text-based interactions closely resemble face-to-face conversation and thus contain many of the linguistic phenomena encountered in natural, spontaneous dialogue. These include self- and other-correction, mid-sentence continuations, interruptions, overlaps, fillers, and hedges. We also present a generic n-gram framework for building user (i.e. tutor) simulations from this type of incremental data, which is freely available to researchers. We show that the simulations produce outputs that are similar to the original data (e.g. 78% turn match similarity). Finally, we train and evaluate a Reinforcement Learning dialogue control agent for learning visually grounded word meanings, trained from the BURCHAK corpus. The learned policy shows comparable performance to a rule-based system built previously.

1 Introduction

Identifying, classifying, and talking about objects and events in the surrounding environment are key capabilities for intelligent, goal-driven systems that interact with other humans and the external world (e.g. robots, smart spaces, and other automated systems). To this end, there has recently been a surge of interest and significant progress made on a variety of related tasks, including generation of Natural Language (NL) descriptions of images, or identifying images based on NL descriptions (Bruni et al., 2014; Socher et al., 2014; Farhadi et al., 2009; Silberer and Lapata, 2014; Sun et al., 2013). Another strand of work has focused on incremental reference resolution in a model where word meaning is modeled as classifiers (the so-called Words-As-Classifiers model (Kennington and Schlangen, 2015)).

T(utor): it is a ... [[sako]] burchak.
L(earner): [[suzuli?]]
T: no, it's sako
L: okay, i see.

(a) Dialogue Example from the corpus

(b) The Chat Tool Window during dialogue in (a) above

Figure 1: Example of turn overlap + subsequent correction in the BURCHAK corpus ('sako' is the invented word for red, 'suzuli' for green and 'burchak' for square)

However, none of this prior work focuses on how concepts/word meanings are *learned and adapted in interactive dialogue* with a human, the most common setting in which robots, home automation devices, smart spaces etc. operate, and, indeed the richest resource that such devices could exploit for adaptation over time to the idiosyncrasies of the language used by their users.

Though recent prior work has focused on the problem of learning visual groundings in interaction with a tutor (see e.g. (Yu et al., 2016b; Yu et

Proceedings of the 6th Workshop on Vision and Language, pages 1–10,
Valencia, Spain, April 4, 2017.

al., 2016a)), it has made use of hand-constructed, synthetic dialogue examples that thus lack in variation, and many of the characteristic, but consequential phenomena observed in naturalistic dialogue (see below). Indeed, to our knowledge, there is no existing data set of real human-human dialogues in this domain, suitable for training multimodal conversational agents that perform the task of *actively learning visual concepts* from a human partner in *natural, spontaneous* dialogue.

(a) Multiple Dialogue Actions in one turn
L: so this shape is wakaki?
T: yes, well done. let's move to the color. So what color is this?
(b) Self-Correction
L: what is this object?
T: this is a sako ... no no ... a suzuli burchak.
(c) Overlapping
T: this color [[is]] ... [[sa]]ko.
L: [[su]]zul[[i?]]
T: no, it's sako.
L: okay.
(d) Continuation
T: what is it called?
L: sako
T: and?
L: aylana.
(e) Fillers
T: what is this object?
L: a sako um... sako wakaki.
T: great job.

Table 1: Dialogue Examples in the Data (L for the learner and T for the tutor)

Natural, spontaneous dialogue is *inherently incremental* (Crocker et al., 2000; Ferreira, 1996; Purver et al., 2009), and thus gives rise to dialogue phenomena such as self- and other-corrections, continuations, unfinished sentences, interruptions and overlaps, hedges, pauses and fillers. These phenomena are interactionally and semantically consequential, and contribute directly to how dialogue partners coordinate their actions and the emergent semantic content of their conversation. They also strongly mediate how a conversational agent might adapt to their partner over time. For example, self-interruption, and subsequent self-correction (see example in table 1.b) as well as hesitations/fillers (see example in table 1.e) aren't simply noise and are used by listeners to guide linguistic processing (Clark and Fox Tree, 2002); similarly, while simultaneous speech is the bane of dialogue system designers, interruptions and subsequent continuations (see examples in table 1.c and 1.d) are performed deliberately by speakers to demonstrate strong levels of understanding (Clark, 1996).

Despite this importance, these phenomena are excluded in many dialogue corpora, and glossed over/removed by state of the art speech recognisers (e.g. Sphinx-4 (Walker et al., 2004) and Google's web-based ASR (Schalkwyk et al., 2010); see Baumann et al. (2016) for a comparison). One reason for this is that naturalistic spoken interaction is excessively expensive and time-consuming to transcribe and annotate on a level of granularity fine-grained enough to reflect the strict time-linear nature of these phenomena.

In this paper, we present a new dialogue data set - the BURCHAK corpus - collected using a new *incremental* variant of the DiET chat-tool (Healey et al., 2003; Mills and Healey, submitted)[1], which enables character-by-character, text-based interaction between pairs of participants, and which circumvents all transcription effort as all this data, including all timing information at the character level is automatically recorded.

The chat-tool is designed to support, elicit, and record at a fine-grained level, dialogues that resemble the face-to-face setting in that turns are: (1) constructed and displayed incrementally as they are typed; (2) transient; (3) potentially overlapping as participants can type at the same time; (4) not editable, i.e. deletion is not permitted - see Sec. 3 and Fig. 2. Thus, we have been able to collect many of the important phenomena mentioned above that arise from the inherently incremental nature of language processing in dialogue - see table 1.

Having presented the data set, we then go on to introduce a generic n-gram framework for building user simulations for either task-oriented or non-task-oriented dialogue systems from this dataset, or others constructed using the same tool. We apply this framework to train a robust user model that is able to simulate the tutor's behaviour to interactively teach (visual) word meanings to a Reinforcement Learning dialogue agent.

[1]Available from `https://sites.google.com/site/hwinteractionlab/babble`

(a) Chat Client Window (Tutor: "it is a ...", Learner: "suzuli?", Tutor: "sako burch")

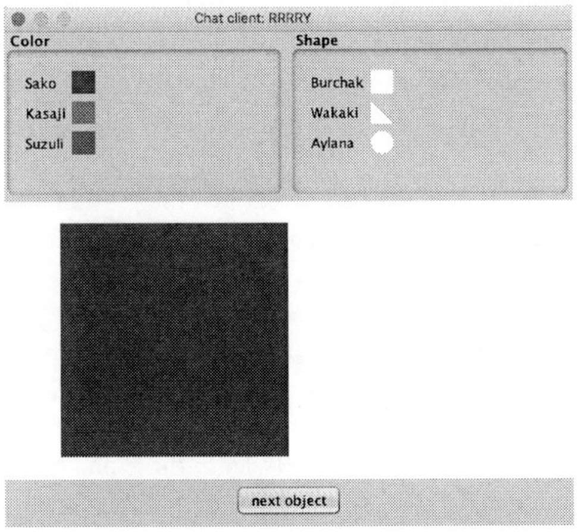

(b) Task Panel for Tutor (Learner only sees the object)

Figure 2: Snapshot of the DiET Chat tool, the Tutor's Interface

2 Related Work

In this section, we will present an overview of relevant data-sets and techniques for Human-Human dialogue collection, as well as approaches to user simulation based on realistic data.

2.1 Human-Human Data Collection

There are several existing corpora of human-human spontaneous spoken dialogue, such as SWITCHBOARD (Godfrey et al., 1992), and the British National Corpus, which consist of open, unrestricted telephone conversations between people, where there are no specific tasks to be achieved. These datasets contain many of the incremental dialogue phenomena that we are interested in, but there is no shared visual scene between participants, meaning we cannot use such data to explore learning of perceptually grounded language. More relevant is the MAPTASK corpus (Thompson et al., 1993), where dialogue participants both have maps which are not shared. This dataset allows investigation of negotiation dialogue, where object names can be agreed, and so does support some work on language grounding. However, in the MAPTASK, grounded word meanings are not taught by ostensive definition as is the case in our new dataset.

We further note that the DiET Chat Tool (Healey et al., 2003; Mills and Healey, submitted) while designed to elicit conversational structures which resemble face-to-face dialogue (see examples in table 1), circumvents the need for the very expensive and time-consuming step of spoken dialogue transcription, but nevertheless produces data at a very fine-grained level. It also includes tools for creating more abstract (e.g. turn-based) representations of conversation.

2.2 User Simulation

Training a dialogue strategy is one of the fundamental tasks of the user simulation. Approaches to user simulation can be categorised based on the level of abstraction at which the dialogue is modeled: 1) the intention-level has become the most popular user model that predicts the next possible user dialogue action according to the dialogue history and the user/task goal (Eckert et al., 1997; Asri et al., 2016; Cuayáhuitl et al., 2005; Chandramohan et al., 2012; Eshky et al., 2012; Ai and Weng, 2008; Georgila et al., 2005); 2) on the word/utterance-level, instead of dialogue action, the user simulation can also be built for predicting the full user utterances or a sequence of words given specific information (Chung, 2004; Schatzmann et al., 2007b); and 3) on the semantic-level, the whole dialogue can be modeled as a sequence of user behaviors in the semantic representation (Schatzmann et al., 2007a; Schatzmann et al., 2007c; Kalatzis et al., 2016).

There are also some user simulations built on multiple levels. For instance, Jung et al. (2009) integrated different data-driven approaches on intention and word levels to build a novel user simulation. The user intent simulation is for generating user intention patterns, and then a two-phase data-driven domain-specific user utterance simulation is proposed to produce a set of structured utterances with sequences of words given a user intent and select the best one using the BLEU score. The user simulation framework we present below is generic in that one can use it to train user simulations on a word-by-word, utterance-by-utterance, or action-by-action levels, and it can be used for both goal-oriented and non-goal-oriented domains.

3 Data Collection using the DiET Chat Tool and a Novel Shape and Colour Learning Task

In this section, we describe our data collection method and process, including the concept learning task given to the human participants.

The DiET experimental toolkit This is a custom-built Java application (Healey et al., 2003; Mills and Healey, submitted) that allows two or more participants to communicate in a shared chat window. It supports live, fine-grained and highly local experimental manipulations of ongoing human-human conversation (see e.g. (Eshghi and Healey, 2015)). The variant we use here supports text-based, character-by-character, interaction between pairs of participants, and here we use it solely for data-collection, where everything that the participants type to each other passes through the DiET server, which transmits the utterance to the other clients on the character level and all are displayed *on the same row/track* in the chat window (see Fig. 2a) - this means that when participants type at the same time in interruptions and turn overlaps, their utterances will be all jumbled up (see Fig. 1b). To simulate the transience of speech in face-to-face conversation with its characteristic phenomena, all utterances in the chat window fade out after 1 second. Furthermore, like in speech, deletes are not permitted: if a character is typed, it cannot be deleted. The chat-tool is thus designed to support, elicit, and record at a fine-grained level, dialogues that resemble face-to-face dialogue in that turns are: (1) constructed and displayed incrementally as they are typed; (2) transient; (3) potentially overlapping; (4) not editable, i.e. deletion is not permitted.

Task and materials The learning/tutoring task given to the participants involves a pair of participants who talk about visual attributes (e.g. colour and shape) through a sequence of 9 visual objects, one at a time. The objects are created based on a 3 x 3 visual attribute matrix (including 3 colours and 3 shapes (see Fig.2b)). This task is assumed in a second-language learning scenario, where each visual attribute, instead of standard English words, is assigned to a new unknown word in a made-up language, e.g. "sako" for red and "burchak" for square: participants are not allowed to use any of the usual colour and shape words from the English language. We design the task in this way to collect data for situations where a robot has to learn the meaning of human visual attribute terms. In such a setting the robot has to learn the perceptual groundings of words such as "red". However, humans already know these groundings, so to collect data about teaching such perceptual meanings, we invented new attribute terms whose groundings the Learner must discover through interaction.

The overall goal of the task is for the learner to identify the shape and colour of the presented objects correctly for as many objects as possible. So the tutor initially needs to teach the learner about these using the presented objects. For this, the tutor is provided with a visual dictionary of the (invented) colour and shape terms (see Fig. 2), but the learner only ever sees the object itself. The learner will thus gradually learn these and be able to identify them, so that initiative in the conversation tends to be reversed on later objects, with the learner making guesses and the tutor either confirming these or correcting them.

Participants Forty participants were recruited from among students and research staff from various disciplines at Heriot-Watt University, including 22 native speakers and 18 non-native speakers.

Procedure The participants in each pair were randomly assigned to experimental roles (Tutor vs. Learner). They were given written instructions about the task and had an opportunity to ask questions about the procedure. They were then seated back-to-back in the same room, each at a desk with a PC displaying the appropriate task window and chat client window (see Fig.2). They were asked to go through all visual objects in at most 30 minutes and then the Learner was assessed to check how many new colour and shape words they had learned. Each participant was paid 10.00 for participation. The best performing pair was also given a 20 Amazon Voucher as prize.

4 The BURCHAK Corpus Statistics

4.1 Overview

Using the above procedure, we have collected 177 dialogues (each about one visual object) with a total of 2454 turns, where a turn is defined[2] as a sequence of consecutive characters typed by a single participant with a delay of no more than 1100 ms

[2]Note that the definition of a 'turn' in an incremental system is somewhat arbitrary.

between the characters. Figure 4a shows the distribution of dialogue length (i.e. number of turns) in the corpus. where the average number of turns per dialogue is 13.86.

4.2 Incremental Dialogue Phenomena

As noted, the DiET Chattool is designed to elicit and record conversations that resemble face-to-face dialogue. In this paper, we report specifically on a variety of dialogue phenomena that arise from the incremental nature of language processing. These are the following:

- **Overlapping**: where interlocutors speak/type at the same time (i.e. the original corpus contains over 800 overlaps), leading to jumbled up text on the DiET interface (see Fig. 1);
- **Self-Correction**: a kind of correction that is performed incrementally in the same turn by a speaker; this can either be conceptual, or simply repairing a misspelling or mispronunciation.
- **Self-Repetition**: the interlocutor repeats words, phrases, even sentences, in the same turn.
- **Continuation (aka Split-Utterance)**: the interlocutor continues the previous utterance (by herself or the other) where either the second part, or the first part or both are syntactically incomplete.
- **Filler**: allows the interlocutor to further plan her utterance while keeping the floor. These can also elicit continuations from the other (Howes et al., 2012). This is performed using tokens such as 'urm', 'err', 'uhh', or '...'.

For annotating self-corrections, self-repetitions and continuations we have loosely followed protocols from Purver et al. (2009; Colman and Healey (2011). Figure 4d shows how frequently these incremental phenomena occur in the BURCHAK Corpus. This figure excludes Overlaps which were much more frequent: 800 in total, which amounts to about 4.5 per dialogue.

4.3 Cleaning up the data for the User Simulation

For the purpose of the annotation of Dialogue Actions, subsequent training of the user simulation, and the Reinforcement Learning described below, we cleaned up the original corpus as follows: 1) we fixed the spelling mistakes which were not repaired by the participants themselves; 2) we also removed snippets of conversation where the participants had misunderstood the task (e.g. trying to describe the objects or where they had used other languages) (see Figure 3); as well as 3) removing emoticons (which frequently occurs in the chat tool).

T: the word for the color is similar to the word for Japanese rice wine. except it ends in o.
L: sake?
T: yup, but end with an o.
L: okay, sako.

Figure 3: Example of Dialogue Snippet with the misunderstanding of the task

We trained a simulated tutor based on this cleaned up data (see below, Section 5).

4.4 Dialogue Actions and their frequencies

The cleaned up data was annotated for the following dialogue actions:

- **Inform**: the action to inform the correct attribute words of an object to the partner, including statement, question-answering, correction, , e.g. "this is a suzuli burchak" or "this is sako";
- **Acknowledgment**: the ability to process confirmations from the *tutor*/the *learner*, e.g. "Yes, it's a square".
- **Rejection**: the ability to process negations from the *tutor*, e.g. "no, it's not red";
- **Asking**: the action to ask WH or polar questions requesting correct information, e.g. "what colour is this?" or "is this a red square?".
- **Focus**: the action to switch the dialogue topic onto specific objects or attributes, e.g. "let's move to shape now";
- **Clarification**: the action to clarify the categories for particular attribute names, e.g. "this is for color not shape";
- **Checking**: the action to check whether the partner understood, e.g. "get it?";
- **Repetition**: the action to request Repetitions to double-check the learned knowledge, e.g. "can you repeat the color again?";

- **Offer-Help**: the action to help the partner answer questions, occurs frequently when the learner cannot answer it immediately, e.g. "L: it is a ... T: need help? L: yes. T: a sako burchak.";

Fig. 4c shows how often each dialogue action occurs in the data set; and Fig. 4b shows the frequencies of these actions by the learner and the tutor individually in each dialogue turn. In contrast with a lot of previous work which assumes a single action per turn, here we get multiple actions per turn (see Table 1) In terms of the *Learner* behavior, the learner mostly performs a single action per turn. On the other hand, although the majority of the dialogue turns on the tutor side also have a single action, about 22.59% of the dialogue turns perform more than one action.

5 TeachBot User Simulation

Here we describe the generic user simulation framework, based on n-grams, for building user simulation from this type of incremental corpus. We apply this framework to train a TeachBot user simulator that is used to train a RL interactive concept learning agent, both here, and in future work. The model is here trained from the cleaned up version of the corpus.

5.1 The N-gram User Simulation

The proposed user model is a compound n-gram simulation that the probability $(P(t|w_1,..,w_n,c_1,..,c_m))$ of an item t (an action or utterance from the tutor in our work) is predicted based on a sequence of the most recent words $(w_1,\ldots,w_n)$ from the previous utterance and additional dialogue context parameters C:

$$P(t|w_1,..,w_n,c_1,..,c_m) = \frac{freq(t,w_1,..,w_n,c_1,..,c_m)}{freq(w_1,..,w_n,c_1,..,c_m)} \quad (1)$$

where $c_1,..,c_m \in C$ represent additional conditions for specific user/task goals (e.g. goal completion as well as previous dialogue context).

For this specific task, the additional dialogue conditions (C) are as follows: (1) the color state (C_{state}) for whether the color attribute is identified correctly, (2) the shape state (S_{state}) for whether the shape attribute is identified correctly, as well as 3) the previous context ($preContxt$) for which attribute (colour or shape) is currently under discussion.

In order to reduce mismatch risk, the simulation model is able to back-off to smaller n-grams when it cannot find any n-grams matched to the current word sequence and conditions. To eliminate the search restriction by the additional conditions, we applied the nearest neighbors algorithm to search for the n-gram matches by calculating the Hamming distance of each pair of n-grams.

The n-gram user simulation is generic, as it is designed to handle the item prediction on multiple levels, on which the predicted item, t, can be assigned either to (1) a full user utterance (U_t) on the utterance level; (2) a combined sequence of dialogue actions (Das_t); or alternatively (3) the next word/lexical token. During the simulation, the n-gram model chooses the next item according to the distribution of n-grams. In terms of the action level, a user utterance will be chosen upon a distribution of utterance templates collected from the corpus and combined given dialogue actions Das_t. The tutor simulation we train here is at the level of the action and utterance, and is evaluated on the same levels below. However, the framework can be used to train to predict fully incrementally on a word-by-word basis. In this case, the $w_i(i < n)$ in Eq.1 will contain not only a sequence of words from the previous system utterance, but also words from the current speaker (the tutor itself as it is generating).

The probability distribution in equation 1 is induced from the corpus using Maximum Likelihood Estimation, where we count how many times each t occurs with any specific combination of the conditions $(w_1,\ldots,w_n,c_1,\ldots,c_m)$ and divide this by the total number of times t occurs (see Eq 1).

5.2 Evaluation of the User Simulation

We evaluate the proposed user simulation based on the turn-level evaluation metrics by (Keizer et al., 2012), in which evaluation is done on a turn-by-turn basis. Evaluation is done based on the cleaned up corpus (see Section 4). We investigate the performance of the user model on two levels: the utterance level and the action level.

The evaluation is done by comparing the distribution of the predicted actions or utterances with the actual distributions in the data. We report two measures: the Accuracy and Kullback-Leibler Divergence (cross-entropy) to quantify how closely the simulated user responses resemble the real user

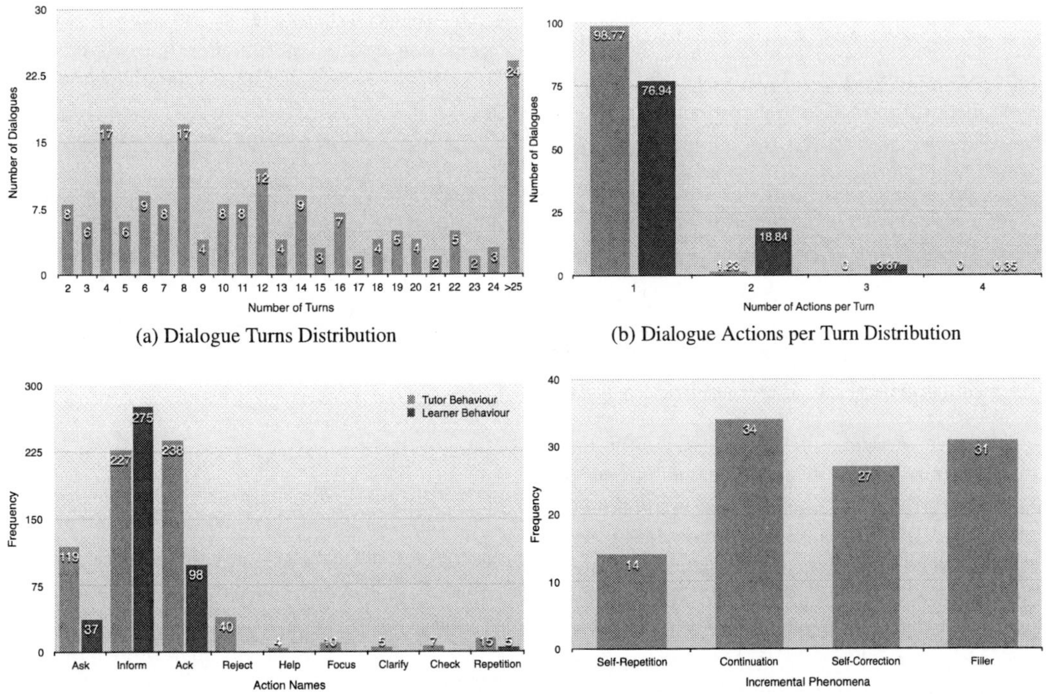

(a) Dialogue Turns Distribution

(b) Dialogue Actions per Turn Distribution

(c) Dialogue Action Frequencies

(d) Incremental Dialogue Phenomena Frequencies

Figure 4: Corpus Statistics

responses in the BURCHAK corpus. Accuracy (Acc) measures the proportion of times an utterance or dialogue act sequence (Das_t) is predicted correctly by the simulator, given a particular set of conditions ($w_1, .., w_n, c_1, .., c_m$). To calculate this, all existing combinations in the data of the values of these variables are tried. If the predicted action or utterance occurs in the data for these given conditions, we count the prediction as correct.

Kullback-Leibler Divergence (KLD) ($D_{kl}(P \parallel Q)$) is applied to compare the predicted distributions and the actual one in the corpus (see Eq.2).

$$D_{kl}(P \parallel Q) = \sum_{i=1}^{M} p_i \log(\frac{p_i}{q_i}) \qquad (2)$$

Table 2 shows the results: the user simulation on both utterance and action levels achieves good performance. The action-based user model, on a more abstract level, would likely be better as it is less sparse, and produces more variation in the resulting utterances.

Ongoing work involves using BURCHAK to train a word-by-word incremental tutor simulation, capable of generating all the incremental phenomena identified earlier.

Simulation	Accuracy (%)	KLD
Utterance-level	77.98	0.2338
Act-level	**84.96**	**0.188**

Table 2: Evaluation of The User Simulation on both Utterance and Act levels

6 Training a prototype concept learning agent from the BURCHAK corpus

In order to demonstrate how the BURCHAK corpus can be used, we train and evaluate a prototype interactive learning agent using Reinforcement Learning (RL) on the collected data. We follow previous task and experiment settings (see (anon, anon)) to compare the learned RL-based agent with a rule-based agent with the best performance from previous work. Instead of using hand-crafted dialogue examples as before, here we train the RL agent in interaction with the user simulation, itself trained from the BURCHAK data as above.

6.1 Experiment Setup

To compare the performance of the rule-based system and the trained RL-based system in the interactive learning process, we follow all experiment setup, including visual data-set and cross-validation method. We also follow the evaluation metrics provided by (2016b) : *Overall Performance Ratio* (R_{perf}) to measures the trade-offs between the cost to the tutor and the accuracy of the learned meanings, i.e. the classifiers that ground our colour and shape concepts. (see Eq.3).

$$R_{perf} = \frac{\Delta Acc}{C_{tutor}} \quad (3)$$

i.e. the increase in accuracy per unit of the cost, or equivalently the gradient of the curve in Fig. 5 We seek dialogue strategies that maximise this.

The cost C_{tutor} measure reflects the effort needed by a human tutor in interacting with the system. Skocaj et. al. (2009) point out that a comprehensive teachable system should learn as autonomously as possible, rather than involving the human tutor too frequently. There are several possible costs that the tutor might incur: C_{inf} refers to the cost (assigned to 5 points) of the tutor providing information on a single attribute concept (e.g. "this is red" or "this is a square"); $C_{ack/rej}$ is the cost (0.5 points) for a simple confirmation (like "yes", "right") or rejection (such as "no"); C_{crt} is the cost of correction (5 points) for a single concept (e.g. "no, it is blue" or "no, it is a circle").

6.2 Results & Discussion

Fig. 5 plots Accuracy against Tutoring Cost directly. The gradient of this curve corresponds to *increase in Accuracy per unit of the Tutoring Cost*: a measure of the trade-off between accuracy of learned meanings and tutoring cost.

The result shows that the RL-based learning agent achieves a comparable performance with the rule-based system.

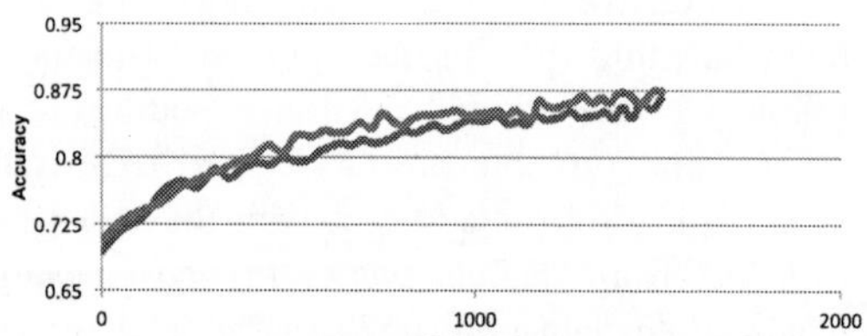

Figure 5: Evolution of Learning Performance

Table 3 shows an example dialogue between the learned concept learning agent and the tutor simulation, where the user model simulates the tutor behaviour (*T*) for the learning tasks. In this example, the utterance produced by the simulation involves two incremental phenomena, i.e. a self-correction and a continuation, though note that these have not been produced on a word-by-word level.

L: so is this shape square?
T: no, it's a squ ... sorry ... a circle. and color?
L: red?
T: yes, good job.

Table 3: Dialogue Example between a Learned Policy and the Simulated Tutor

7 Conclusion

We presented a new data collection tool, a new data set, and and associated dialogue simulation framework which focuses on visual language grounding and natural, incremental dialogue phenomena. The tools and data are freely available and easy to use.

We have collected new human-human dialogue data on visual attribute learning tasks, which are then used to create a generic n-gram user simulation for future research and development. We used this n-gram user model to train and evaluate an optimized dialogue policy, which learns grounded word meanings from a human tutor, incrementally, over time. This dialogue policy optimisation learns a complete dialogue control policy from the data, in contrast to earlier work (Yu et al., 2016b) which only optimised confidence thresholds, and where dialogue control was entirely rule-based.

Ongoing work further uses the data and simulation framework here to train a word-by-word incremental tutor simulation, with which to learn complete, incremental dialogue policies, i.e. policies that choose system output at the lexical level (Eshghi and Lemon, 2014). To deal with uncertainty this system in addition takes all the visual classifiers' confidence levels directly as features in a continuous space MDP.

Acknowledgments

This research is supported by the EPSRC, under grant number EP/M01553X/1 (BABBLE project[3]), and by the European Union's Horizon 2020 research and innovation programme under grant agreement No. 688147 (MuMMER project[4]).

[3]https://sites.google.com/site/hwinteractionlab/babble

[4]http://mummer-project.eu/

References

Hua Ai and Fuliang Weng. 2008. User simulation as testing for spoken dialog systems. In *Proceedings of the SIGDIAL 2008 Workshop, The 9th Annual Meeting of the Special Interest Group on Discourse and Dialogue, 19-20 June 2008, Ohio State University, Columbus, Ohio, USA*, pages 164–171.

Layla El Asri, Jing He, and Kaheer Suleman. 2016. A sequence-to-sequence model for user simulation in spoken dialogue systems. *CoRR*, abs/1607.00070.

Timo Baumann, Casey Kennington, Julian Hough, and David Schlangen. 2016. Recognising conversational speech: What an incremental asr should do for a dialogue system and how to get there. In *International Workshop on Dialogue Systems Technology (IWSDS) 2016*. Universität Hamburg.

Elia Bruni, Nam-Khanh Tran, and Marco Baroni. 2014. Multimodal distributional semantics. *J. Artif. Intell. Res.(JAIR)*, 49(1–47).

Senthilkumar Chandramohan, Matthieu Geist, Fabrice Lefevre, and Olivier Pietquin. 2012. Behavior specific user simulation in spoken dialogue systems. In *Speech Communication; 10. ITG Symposium; Proceedings of*, pages 1–4. VDE.

Grace Chung. 2004. Developing a flexible spoken dialog system using simulation. In *Proceedings of the 42nd Annual Meeting of the Association for Computational Linguistics, 21-26 July, 2004, Barcelona, Spain.*, pages 63–70.

Herbert H. Clark and Jean E. Fox Tree. 2002. Using *uh* and *um* in spontaneous speaking. *Cognition*, 84(1):73–111.

Herbert H. Clark. 1996. *Using Language*. Cambridge University Press.

M. Colman and P. G. T. Healey. 2011. The distribution of repair in dialogue. In *Proceedings of the 33rd Annual Meeting of the Cognitive Science Society*, pages 1563–1568, Boston, MA.

Matthew Crocker, Martin Pickering, and Charles Clifton, editors. 2000. *Architectures and Mechanisms in Sentence Comprehension*. Cambridge University Press.

Heriberto Cuayáhuitl, Steve Renals, Oliver Lemon, and Hiroshi Shimodaira. 2005. Human-computer dialogue simulation using hidden markov models. In *IEEE Workshop on Automatic Speech Recognition and Understanding, 2005.*, pages 290–295. IEEE.

Wieland Eckert, Esther Levin, and Roberto Pieraccini. 1997. User modeling for spoken dialogue system evaluation. In *Automatic Speech Recognition and Understanding, 1997. Proceedings., 1997 IEEE Workshop on*, pages 80–87. IEEE.

Arash Eshghi and Patrick G. T. Healey. 2015. Collective contexts in conversation: Grounding by proxy. *Cognitive Science*, pages 1–26.

Arash Eshghi and Oliver Lemon. 2014. How domain-general can we be? learning incremental dialogue systems without dialogue acts. In *Proceedings of SemDial.*

Aciel Eshky, Ben Allison, and Mark Steedman. 2012. Generative goal-driven user simulation for dialog management. In *Proceedings of the 2012 Joint Conference on Empirical Methods in Natural Language Processing and Computational Natural Language Learning, EMNLP-CoNLL 2012, July 12-14, 2012, Jeju Island, Korea*, pages 71–81.

Ali Farhadi, Ian Endres, Derek Hoiem, and David Forsyth. 2009. Describing objects by their attributes. In *Proceedings of the IEEE Computer Society Conference on Computer Vision and Pattern Recognition (CVPR.*

Victor Ferreira. 1996. Is it better to give than to donate? Syntactic flexibility in language production. *Journal of Memory and Language*, 35:724–755.

Kallirroi Georgila, James Henderson, and Oliver Lemon. 2005. Learning user simulations for information state update dialogue systems. In *INTERSPEECH 2005 - Eurospeech, 9th European Conference on Speech Communication and Technology, Lisbon, Portugal, September 4-8, 2005*, pages 893–896.

John J. Godfrey, Edward Holliman, and J. McDaniel. 1992. SWITCHBOARD: Telephone speech corpus for research and development. In *Proceedings of IEEE ICASSP-92*, pages 517–520, San Francisco, CA.

P. G. T. Healey, Matthew Purver, James King, Jonathan Ginzburg, and Greg Mills. 2003. Experimenting with clarification in dialogue. In *Proceedings of the 25th Annual Meeting of the Cognitive Science Society*, Boston, Massachusetts, August.

Christine Howes, Patrick G. T. Healey, Matthew Purver, and Arash Eshghi. 2012. Finishing each other's ... responding to incomplete contributions in dialogue. In *Proceedings of the 34th Annual Meeting of the Cognitive Science Society (CogSci 2012)*, pages 479–484, Sapporo, Japan, August.

Sangkeun Jung, Cheongjae Lee, Kyungduk Kim, Minwoo Jeong, and Gary Geunbae Lee. 2009. Data-driven user simulation for automated evaluation of spoken dialog systems. *Computer Speech & Language*, 23(4):479–509.

Dimitrios Kalatzis, Arash Eshghi, and Oliver Lemon. 2016. Bootstrapping incremental dialogue systems: using linguistic knowledge to learn from minimal data. In *Proceedings of the NIPS 2016 workshop on Learning Methods for Dialogue*, Barcelona.

Simon Keizer, Stphane Rossignol, Senthilkumar Chandramohan, and Olivier Pietquin. 2012. User Simulation in the Development of Statistical Spoken Dialogue Systems. In Oliver Lemon Olivier Pietquin, editor, *Data-Driven Methods for Adaptive Spoken Dialogue Systems: Computational Learning for Conversational Interfaces*, chapter 4, pages 39–73. Springer, November.

Casey Kennington and David Schlangen. 2015. Simple learning and compositional application of perceptually grounded word meanings for incremental reference resolution. In *Proceedings of the Conference for the Association for Computational Linguistics (ACL-IJCNLP)*. Association for Computational Linguistics.

Gregory J. Mills and Patrick G. T. Healey. submitted. The Dialogue Experimentation toolkit. *xx*, (?).

Matthew Purver, Christine Howes, Eleni Gregoromichelaki, and Patrick G. T. Healey. 2009. Split utterances in dialogue: A corpus study. In *Proceedings of the 10th Annual SIGDIAL Meeting on Discourse and Dialogue (SIGDIAL 2009 Conference)*, pages 262–271, London, UK, September. Association for Computational Linguistics.

Johan Schalkwyk, Doug Beeferman, Franoise Beaufays, Bill Byrne, Ciprian Chelba, Mike Cohen, Maryam Kamvar, and Brian Strope. 2010. "Your word is my command": Google search by voice: A case study. In *Advances in Speech Recognition: Mobile Environments, Call Centers and Clinics*, chapter 4, pages 61–90. Springer, New York.

Jost Schatzmann, Blaise Thomson, Karl Weilhammer, Hui Ye, and Steve J. Young. 2007a. Agenda-based user simulation for bootstrapping a POMDP dialogue system. In *Human Language Technology Conference of the North American Chapter of the Association of Computational Linguistics, Proceedings, April 22-27, 2007, Rochester, New York, USA*, pages 149–152.

Jost Schatzmann, Blaise Thomson, and Steve J. Young. 2007b. Error simulation for training statistical dialogue systems. In *IEEE Workshop on Automatic Speech Recognition & Understanding, ASRU 2007, Kyoto, Japan, December 9-13, 2007*, pages 526–531.

Jost Schatzmann, Blaise Thomson, and Steve J. Young. 2007c. Statistical user simulation with a hidden agenda. In *Proceedings of the SIGDIAL 2007 Workshop, The 9th Annual Meeting of the Special Interest Group on Discourse and Dialogue, 1-2 September 2007, the University of Antwerp, Belgium.*

Carina Silberer and Mirella Lapata. 2014. Learning grounded meaning representations with autoencoders. In *Proceedings of the 52nd Annual Meeting of the Association for Computational Linguistics (Volume 1: Long Papers)*, volume 1, pages 721–732, Baltimore, Maryland, June. Association for Computational Linguistics.

Danijel Skočaj, Matej Kristan, and Aleš Leonardis. 2009. Formalization of different learning strategies in a continuous learning framework. In *Proceedings of the Ninth International Conference on Epigenetic Robotics; Modeling Cognitive Development in Robotic Systems*, pages 153–160. Lund University Cognitive Studies.

Richard Socher, Andrej Karpathy, Quoc V Le, Christopher D Manning, and Andrew Y Ng. 2014. Grounded compositional semantics for finding and describing images with sentences. *Transactions of the Association for Computational Linguistics*, 2:207–218.

Yuyin Sun, Liefeng Bo, and Dieter Fox. 2013. Attribute based object identification. In *Robotics and Automation (ICRA), 2013 IEEE International Conference on*, pages 2096–2103. IEEE.

Henry S. Thompson, Anne Anderson, Ellen Gurman Bard, Gwyneth Doherty-Sneddon, Alison Newlands, and Cathy Sotillo. 1993. The hcrc map task corpus: Natural dialogue for speech recognition. In *Proceedings of the Workshop on Human Language Technology*, HLT '93, pages 25–30, Stroudsburg, PA, USA. Association for Computational Linguistics.

Willie Walker, Paul Lamere, Philip Kwok, Bhiksha Raj, Rita Singh, Evandro Gouvea, Peter Wolf, and Joe Woelfel. 2004. Sphinx-4: A flexible open source framework for speech recognition. Technical report, Mountain View, CA, USA.

Yanchao Yu, Arash Eshghi, and Oliver Lemon. 2016a. Incremental generation of visually grounded language in situated dialogue. In *Proceedings of INLG 2016*.

Yanchao Yu, Arash Eshghi, and Oliver Lemon. 2016b. Training an adaptive dialogue policy for interactive learning of visually grounded word meanings. In *Proceedings of the SIGDIAL 2016 Conference, The 17th Annual Meeting of the Special Interest Group on Discourse and Dialogue, 13-15 September 2016, Los Angeles, CA, USA*, pages 339–349.

The Use of Object Labels and Spatial Prepositions as Keywords in a Web-Retrieval-Based Image Caption Generation System

Brandon Birmingham and **Adrian Muscat**
Communications & Computer Engineering
University of Malta
Msida MSD 2080, Malta
{brandon.birmingham.12, adrian.muscat}@um.edu.mt

Abstract

In this paper, a retrieval-based caption generation system that searches the web for suitable image descriptions is studied. Google's search-by-image is used to find potentially relevant web multimedia content for query images. Sentences are extracted from web pages and the likelihood of the descriptions is computed to select one sentence from the retrieved text documents. The search mechanism is modified to replace the caption generated by Google with a caption composed of labels and spatial prepositions as part of the query's text alongside the image. The object labels are obtained using an off-the-shelf R-CNN and a machine learning model is developed to predict the prepositions. The effect on the caption generation system performance when using the generated text is investigated. Both human evaluations and automatic metrics are used to evaluate the retrieved descriptions. Results show that the web-retrieval-based approach performed better when describing single-object images with sentences extracted from stock photography websites. On the other hand, images with two image objects were better described with template-generated sentences composed of object labels and prepositions.

1 Introduction

The automatic generation of concise natural language descriptions for images is currently gaining immense popularity in both Computer Vision and Natural Language Processing communities (Bernardi et al., 2016). The general process of automatically describing an image fundamentally involves the visual analysis of the image content such that a succinct natural language statement, verbalising the most salient image features, can be generated. In addition, natural language generation methods are needed to construct linguistically and grammatically correct sentences. Describing image content is very useful in applications for image retrieval based on detailed and specific image descriptions, caption generation to enhance the accessibility of current and existing image collections and most importantly as an assistive technology for visually impaired people (Kulkarni et al., 2011). Research work on automatic image description generation can be organised in three categories (Bernardi et al., 2016). The first group generates textual descriptions from scratch by analysing the composition of an image in terms of image objects, attributes, scene types and event actions, extracted from image visual features. The other groups describe images by retrieving sentences either from *visual* space composed of image-description pairs or from a *multimodal* space that combines image and sentences in one single space. As opposed to direct-generation-based methods, the latter two approaches generate less verbose and more human-like descriptions. In this paper, a web-retrieval-based system that exploits the ever-growing vision-text content is studied while exploring how object labels and prepositions affect the retrieval of image descriptions.

This paper is organised as follows: section 2 gives an overview of existing image caption algorithms. Section 3 outlines the problem definition and section 4 presents a web-retrieval-based framework followed by its implementation details in section 5. The dataset and evaluation are discussed in sections 6 and 7 respectively. The results are presented in section 8 followed by a discussion in section 9. Finally, section 10 concludes with the main observations and the future direction.

Proceedings of the 6th Workshop on Vision and Language, pages 11–20,
Valencia, Spain, April 4, 2017.

2 Related Work

Direct-generation models (Fang et al., 2015; Kulkarni et al., 2011; Li et al., 2011; Yang et al., 2011), exploit the image visual information to derive an image description by driving a natural language generation model such as *n*-grams, templates and grammar rules. Despite producing correct and relevant image descriptions, this approach tends to generate verbose and non-human-like image captions. The second and most relevant group of models to this paper, tackles the problem of textually describing an image as a *retrieval* problem. There are attempts that make use of pre-associated text or meta-data to describe images. For instance, Feng and Lapata (2010) generated captions for news images using an extractive and abstractive generation methods that require relevant text documents as input to the model. Similarly, Aker and Gaizauskas (2010) relied on GPS metadata to access relevant text documents to be able to generate captions for geo-tagged images. Other models formulate descriptions by finding visually similar images to the query images from a collection of already-annotated images. Query images are then described either by (a) reusing the whole description of the most visually similar retrieved image, or by (b) associating relevant phrases from a large collection of image and description pairs (Ordonez et al., 2016). Retrieval models can be further subdivided, based on the technique used for representing and computing image similarity. The first subgroup uses a *visual space* for finding related images, while the second subgroup uses a *multimodal space* for combining both textual and visual image information. The first subgroup (Ordonez et al., 2011; Ordonez et al., 2016; Gupta et al., 2012; Mason and Charniak, 2014; Yagcioglu et al., 2015), is intended to first extract visual features from the query images. Based on a visual similarity measure dependent on the extracted features, a candidate set of related images is retrieved from a large collection of pre-annotated images. Retrieved descriptions are then re-ranked by further exploiting the visual and textual information extracted from the retrieved candidate set of similar images. Conversely, retrieving descriptions from a multimodal space is characterised by the joint space between visual and textual data constructed from a collection of image-description pairs. For example, in Farhadi et al. (2010), image descriptions were retrieved from a multimodal space consisting of $< object, action, scene >$ tuples. More recently, deep neural networks were introduced to map images and corresponding descriptions in one joint multimodal space (Socher et al., 2014; Kiros et al., 2014; Donahue et al., 2015; Karpathy and Li, 2015; Chen and Zitnick, 2015).

3 Problem Definition

Image caption generators are designed to associate images with corresponding sentences, hence they can be viewed in terms of an affinity function $f(i, s)$ that measures the degree of correlation between images and sentences. Based on a set of candidate images $\mathbf{I}_{cand}$ annotated with corresponding candidate sentences $\mathbf{S}_{cand}$, typical retrieval-based caption generation methods describe an image by reusing sentence $s \in \mathbf{S}_{cand}$. The selected sentence is the one that maximises the affinity function $f(i_q, s)$ for a given query image i_q. On the contrary, generation-based image descriptors attempt to construct a novel sentence s_n composed of image entities and attributes.

The system described in this paper extracts sentences from a collection of web pages $\mathbf{W}$, rather than from a limited set of candidate human-authored image descriptions $\mathbf{S}_{cand}$, as done in most existing retrieval-based studies. Websites containing visually similar images to the query image are found using search-by-image technology. The intuition to this method is based on the fact that the evergrowing Internet-based multimedia data is a readily-available data source as opposed to the purposely constructed and limited image-description datasets used in many studies. The search for a query image can be thought of as providing a dynamic and specialised small dataset for a given query image.

The suggested framework starts by generating a simple image description based on the image visual entities and their spatial relationship. This simple description is then used as keywords to drive and optimise a web-data-driven based retrieval process. The latter is primarily intended to retrieve the most relevant sentence from the set of candidate web pages $\mathbf{W}$ by utilising the functionality offered by a search-by-image algorithm. This strategy is adopted under the assumption that web pages featuring visually similar images to a query image i_q, can contain sentences which can be effectively re-used to describe image i_q.

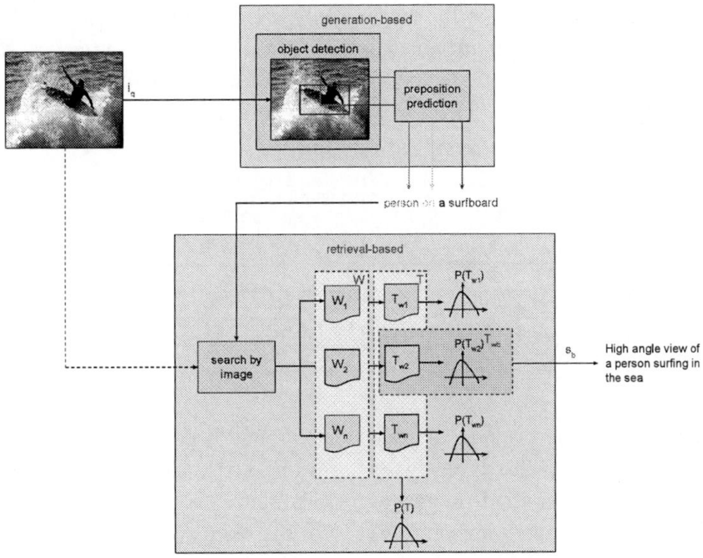

Figure 1: The proposed web-retrieval-based system designed in two stages. The query image i_q is first described by the keywords generated by the first stage. These are then used to retrieve image descriptions from a collection of web pages $\mathbf{W}$. The best sentence s_b is extracted from the best text document $\mathbf{T}_{w_b}$, with respect to the global word probability distribution $P(\mathbf{T})$ and the query image i_q.

4 Image Description Framework

The proposed generation-retrieval-based approach is centrally decomposed into two phases. The first *generation* stage of the framework is mainly intended to generate simple image descriptions that will serve as keywords for the second *retrieval* phase. By exploiting the vast amount of image-text data found on the Web, the latter will then extract the most likely sentence for a given query image. A high-level overview of the proposed image description framework is presented in Figure 1.

4.1 Generation-based Image Description

The first stage of the image description generation framework analyses the image visual content and detects the most important image objects. Therefore, the aim of this step is to detect and annotate image objects with corresponding high-level image labels and corresponding bounding boxes. In order to describe the spatial relationship between the predominant image objects, various predictive models based on different textual and geometric feature sets, were investigated as described in section 4.2. From this simple generated image description, in the form of an *object-preposition-article-object* keyword structure, the framework is then designed to drive a web-retrieval-based process. This process exploits both the visual aspect of the query image, as well as the linguistic keywords generated by the first stage of the pipeline.

4.2 Preposition Predictive Model

The generation of prepositions was cast as a prediction-based problem through geometrical and encoded textual features. Four different predictive models based on separate feature sets were analysed. This experiment confirmed that the Random Forest model obtained the best preposition prediction accuracy rate. This was achieved when predicting prepositions via word2vec (Mikolov et al., 2013) textual labels combined with the geometric feature sets used by Muscat and Belz (2015) and Ramisa et al. (2015). This setup marginally outperformed the best preposition prediction accuracy achieved by Ramisa et al. (2015) when trained and evaluated on the same Visen's MSCOCO Prepositions[1] testing set having original object labels. Results can be found in Table 1.

4.3 Retrieval-based Image Description

The aim of the second phase of the proposed framework is to retrieve descriptions based on the visual aspect of a query image and its correspond-

[1] `http://preposition.github.io`

Table 1: The accuracies obtained from the Visen's MSCOCO original object labels. The accuracies for different configuration setups are presented, based on different geometric feature sets, in relation to different textual label encoding. LE stands for the Label Encoder which encodes object labels with corresponding integers, IV for Indicator Vectors and W2V for Word2Vec.

	Geometric + Textual Features											
	Ramisa et al.				Muscat & Belz				All Geometric Features			
Model	LE	IV	W2V	GF	LE	IV	W2V	GF	LE	IV	W2V	GF
SVM	0.03	0.42	0.77	0.60	0.01	0.42	0.77	0.60	0.08	0.44	0.74	0.63
Decision Tree	0.53	0.66	0.75	0.69	0.52	0.65	0.76	0.67	0.53	0.64	0.75	0.69
Random Forest	0.60	0.65	**0.81**	0.72	0.56	0.62	**0.81**	0.69	0.59	0.68	**0.82**	0.71
Logistic Regression	0.64	0.50	0.80	0.64	0.61	0.50	0.81	0.61	0.65	0.51	0.80	0.64

ing simple generated image description, as discussed in Section 4.1. This phase is designed to find a set of web pages composed of images that are visually related to the query image. This search functionality is freely available by the current two dominant search-engines, Google[2] and Bing[3]. These two proprietary image-search algorithms are able to retrieve visually similar images, which may therefore be used for collecting web pages with featured visually similar images. From the retrieved collection of web pages characterised with visually similar images to the query image, this phase is designed to extract the best sentence that can be used to describe the query image. Based on the idea that websites usually describe or discuss the embedded images, it is assumed that this stage is capable of finding human-like sentences describing the incorporated images which can be re-used to describe the query images.

Given a collection of candidate web pages $\mathbf{W}$ with embedded visually similar images, this phase is intended to extract the main text $\mathbf{T}_{w_i}$ from each corresponding web page $w_i \in \mathbf{W}$. This is carried out by analysing the Document Object Model (DOM) of each web page as well as by statistically distinguishing between HTML and textual data. Moreover, this stage is intended to discard any boilerplate text that is normally found in web pages, including navigational text and advertisements by exploiting shallow text features (Kohlschütter et al., 2010). After transforming the set of web pages $\mathbf{W}$ to the corresponding text documents $\mathbf{T}$, this stage computes the word probability distribution $P(\mathbf{T}_{w_i})$ for each $\mathbf{T}_{w_i}$, disregarding any stop words in the distribution. The text found in each text document $\mathbf{T}_{w_i}$ is combined in one text collection $\mathbf{T}$ and the probability distribution $P(\mathbf{T})$, representing all the probabilities for the words contained in collection $\mathbf{T}$, is calculated. The top k most probable words from each generated probability distribution $P(\mathbf{T}_{w_i})$ are considered to find the most probable relevant text document $\mathbf{T}_{w_b}$, for the extraction of the best sentence s_b that describes the query image i_q. Specifically, the best text document is selected by the following maximising function over each text document probability distribution $P(\mathbf{T}_{w_i})$, with respect to the global word probability distribution $P(\mathbf{T})$:

$$\mathbf{T}_{w_b} = \arg\max_{w_i} \sum_{n=1}^{k} P(\mathbf{T}_{w_{i,n}}) P(\mathbf{T} = \mathbf{T}_{w_{i,n}}), \tag{1}$$

where n represents the nth most probable word of the probability distribution.

This strategy is used to eliminate documents that are probably irrelevant to provide correct descriptions for query images. A similar approach is carried out to retrieve the best sentence s_b that could potentially describe the query image. The technique used to select the most appropriate sentence from $\mathbf{T}_{w_b}$ is initiated by extracting the set of candidate sentences $\mathbf{S}_{cand}$ from the selected best file $\mathbf{T}_{w_b}$. The second step is to weight each sentence $s_i \in \mathbf{S}_{cand}$ by the summation over how probable each word is, with respect to the global word probability distribution $P(\mathbf{T})$. Therefore, s_b is retrieved by maximising the following formula:

$$s_b = \arg\max_{s_i} \sum_{n=1}^{|s_i|} P(\mathbf{T} = s_{i,n}), \tag{2}$$

where n represents the nth word found in sentence $s_i \in \mathbf{S}_{cand}$ extracted from the best file

[2]https://images.google.com

[3]https://www.bing.com/images/explore?FORM=ILPSTR

$\mathbf{T}_{w_b}$, and $|s_i|$ represents the number of words found in sentence s_i.

To further enhance the contextual reliability of the selected sentence, the approach used to retrieve image descriptions is combined with the image visual aspect. This is accomplished by weighting the visible object class labels in accordance to their corresponding image predominance level. The area of the visible image entities, with respect to the entire query image i_q, was used to prioritise visible image objects. Therefore, the best sentence s_b is retrieved by combining the knowledge extracted from the most probable words found in $P(\mathbf{T})$ and the visual aspect of the query image i_q, by the following formula:

$$s_b = \arg\max_{s_i} \sum_{n=1}^{|s_i|} P(\mathbf{T} = s_{i,n}) R(i_q, s_{i,n}), \quad (3)$$

where R is a function which computes the area of the object class label $s_{i,n}$ found in the nth word of sentence s_i in the context of image i_q.

5 Implementation

The image description generation framework was modularised and implemented in two stages. To detect the main image objects, the first stage employs the two-phased fast region-based convolutional neural network (R-CNN) proposed by Ren et al. (2015). The first module of the R-CNN is a deep fully convolutional neural network designed to propose regions, while the second module is a detector that uses the proposed regions for detecting image objects enclosed in bounding boxes. This architecture is trained end-to-end into a single network by sharing convolutional features. The deep VGG-16 model (Simonyan and Zisserman, 2014) pre-trained on MSCOCO (Lin et al., 2014) dataset, was utilised to detect image objects with corresponding class labels and bounding boxes. These were then used to infer the spatial relationship between the detected image objects as discussed in section 4.2.

By using the linguistic keywords generated from the first stage, the second part of the framework is designed to retrieve the most probable sentence from a set of relevant web pages that feature visually similar images. The set of web pages is collected by using the free functionality offered by Google's Search By Image[4] proprietary technology. For a given uploaded query image, this functionality is intended to return visually similar images. Based on extracted image visual features and automatically generated textual keywords by the same functionality, Google's Search by Image retrieves visually similar images. The websites of the visually returned images are then retrieved from the corresponding URLs binded with each visually similar image. By using Selenium[5] to automate the headless PhantomJS browser, query images were automatically uploaded to retrieve websites featuring visually similar images. In this study, it was shown how object labels connected with spatial prepositions affect the retrieval search performed by Google's search-by-image algorithm. This was accomplished by replacing Google's keywords with object labels and preposition generated by the first stage of the proposed framework. Furthermore, this study also investigated whether stock photography websites could improve the retrieval search of the designed framework. The retrieval of websites featuring stock photos was achieved by concatenating the phrase "stock photos" with the keywords extracted from the visual aspect of the query image. To detect and extract the main textual content of each respective web page, the boilerpipe[6] toolkit was employed. From the set of extracted text documents, the most probable sentence that best describes the query image is then retrieved, as discussed in Section 4.3.

6 Dataset

To evaluate the proposed image description framework, a specific subset of human-annotated images featured in MSCOCO[7] testing set was used. Since the preposition prediction task is targeted to generate prepositions between two image objects, describing images having exactly two image objects was of particular interest to this study. Therefore, the following steps were carried out to select images consisting of two image objects. From the ViSen's MSCOCO testing set, 1975 instances having strictly one single preposition between two image objects were found and extracted. Finally, 1000 images were randomly selected from the latter subset. Since images may contain background image objects, the same object detector employed in the proposed framework was used for detecting

[4]https://images.google.com

[5]http://docs.seleniumhq.org

[6]https://boilerpipe-web.appspot.com

[7]http://mscoco.org

Table 2: Configuration Setups

Setup	Name	Image Descriptions
G	Generation	Descriptions consisting of object labels
GP	Generation-Preposition	Descriptions consisting of object labels connected with spatial prepositions
R	Retrieval	Descriptions retrieved based on Google's automatic generated keywords
GR	Generation-Retrieval	Descriptions retrieved based on the generated keywords by G
GRS	Generation-Retrieval-Stock	Descriptions retrieved based on the generated keywords by G from stock photography websites
GPR	Generation-Preposition-Retrieval	Description retrieved based on the generated keywords by GP
GPRS	Generation-Preposition-Retrieval-Stock	Descriptions retrieved from stock photography websites based on the descriptions generated by GP

objects. The fast R-CNN found 128 images containing one image object, 438 images containing exactly two image objects, while the remaining 434 images contained more than two image objects. For the evaluation of this framework, images composed of one and two image objects were only considered. Therefore, the framework was evaluated on a dataset consisting of 566 images, where 128 images contain one single object, while the other remaining 438 images contain exactly two image objects.

7 Evaluation

Both human and computational evaluation were used to evaluate the web-retrieval-based framework. The automatic evaluation was performed by using existing metrics, intended to measure the similarity between generated descriptions and corresponding human ground truth descriptions. The measures include BLEU (Papineni et al., 2002), ROUGE_L (Lin and Hovy, 2003), METEOR (Denkowski and Lavie, 2014) and CIDEr (Vedantam et al., 2015). To complement the automatic evaluation, human judgments for image descriptions were obtained from a qualified English teacher. Since the human evaluation process is considerably time-consuming, human judgments were collected for a sample of 200 images split equally for single and double-object images. The same human evaluation criteria proposed by Mitchell et al. (2012) was used to evaluate the generated descriptions. Human evaluation was conducted by rating the grammar, main aspects, correctness, order and the human-likeness of descriptions using a five-point Likert scale.

8 Results

The framework was evaluated in each phase of its pipeline as described in Table 2. The results are given in Tables 3 and 4 for single and double-object images respectively. The generation phase of the framework that describes images with just object labels is represented by G, while the standalone retrieval-based approach which uses Google's automatic generated keywords is represented by R. Furthermore, when describing single-object images, the joint generation-retrieval stage that uses the prototype's keywords is represented by GR. When describing double-object images, the generation-retrieval process is denoted by GPR given that it uses both object labels and prepositions as keywords. Moreover, the results obtained when the retrieval phase considers stock photography websites are denoted by the letter S. The retrieval-based stages are specified by the two parameters, W and F. The latter represents the number of text files analysed from the corresponding websites, whereas W represents the number of most probable words used for the selection of the best sentence from a set of web pages. A grid search was performed to find these parameters for each configuration. The same notation was used for the human evaluation results. Typical image descriptions generated by the proposed web-retrieval-based image caption generation system can be found in Figure 2.

9 Discussion

The automatic evaluation showed that single-object images were best described by the generation-retrieval from stock photography websites (GRS). This outperformed the one-word description of the generation-based configuration

Table 3: Automatic evaluation of single-object images.

Metric	Model			
	G	R (20W, 30F)	GR (5W, 35F)	GRS (5W, 35F)
CIDEr	0.134	0.066	0.099	**0.154**
BLEU@4	0.000	0.000	0.010	**0.013**
BLEU@3	0.000	0.007	0.022	**0.032**
BLEU@2	0.001	0.026	0.058	**0.074**
BLEU@1	0.001	0.080	0.148	**0.173**
ROUGE_L	0.124	0.101	0.133	**0.164**
METEOR	0.062	0.060	0.078	**0.089**

Table 4: Automatic Evaluation of double-object images.

Metric	Model						
	G	GP	R (20W, 30F)	GR (5W, 35F)	GRS (5W, 25F)	GPR (10W, 15F)	GPRS (10W, 15F)
CIDEr	0.482	**0.604**	0.082	0.148	0.176	0.132	0.152
BLEU@4	0.033	**0.132**	0.005	0.014	0.018	0.013	0.017
BLEU@3	0.085	**0.187**	0.015	0.030	0.036	0.028	0.035
BLEU@2	0.165	**0.241**	0.038	0.069	0.081	0.067	0.077
BLEU@1	0.252	**0.292**	0.125	0.190	0.199	0.175	0.190
ROUGE_L	0.340	**0.413**	0.130	0.185	0.210	0.174	0.198
METEOR	0.152	**0.177**	0.078	0.109	0.117	0.100	0.113

(G), as well as the retrieval-based (R) setup. The latter result confirms that the replacement of Google's Search by Image captions improved the retrieved descriptions. This concludes that more relevant images were returned by Google when replacing its automatic caption with object labels.

Conversely, double-object images were best described via the generation-preposition (GP) configuration. Although replacing Google's Search By Image keywords improved the results, the simple descriptions based on object labels connected with spatial prepositions were more accurate. Automatic evaluation also confirmed that the web-retrieval approach (GRS) performs better on double-object images. This study also showed that the retrieval process performs better without using prepositions as keywords. This resulted from the fact that prepositions constrain the search result performed by Google when indexing web pages, since most descriptive text available on the Web includes verbs rather than prepositions.

The human evaluation results for the single-object images are presented in Table 5. Particularly, generation-based (G) descriptions obtained a grammatical median score of 1, confirming that one-word descriptions do not produce grammatically correct sentences. The results also confirm that the used object detector accurately describes the dominant objects in an image. By considering the improbability of one-word human derived descriptions, this stage resulted in a low human likeness score of 2. The retrieval method applied on stock photography websites (RS) lead to grammatical improvement in the generated descriptions. Such descriptions were grammatically rated with a median score of 3. However, results show that the retrieval method decreases the relevancy of the retrieved descriptions. Despite generating grammatically sound sentences with better human-likeness, the human evaluation showed a degree of inconsistency between the descriptions and their corresponding images. When combining the generation (G) and retrieval (RS) proposed approaches, the grammar, order and the human likeness improved for single-object images.

Table 5 also demonstrates that the generation-preposition (GP) configuration generated the best descriptions when describing double-object images. Furthermore, these results also confirmed that the retrieval (RS) approach improves when replacing Google's caption with object labels. The human evaluation also established the ineffectiveness of the retrieval stage when combined with the generation-prepositions (GPRS) stage. This table also confirmed that the web-retrieval approach described double-object images better than single-object images.

Vase and clock in a window sill. | Person launching a kite. | High angle view of a person surfing in the sea. | A shot of a kitchen microwave oven. | Person on skateboard skateboarding in action sport.

(a)

Cat chasing a mouse. | Young person jogging outdoor in nature. | Person sleeping. | Dog in hat. | italy, gressoney, person jumping ski, low angle view.

(b)

Figure 2: (a) Correct and (b) incorrect descriptions generated by the web-retrieval-based framework.

Table 5: Human evaluation of single and double-object images with scores (1-5) obtained for each stage of the proposed framework: median, mean and standard deviation in parentheses.

	single-object images				
Model	Grammar	Main Aspects	Correctness	Order	Humanlike
G	1 (1.11, 0.31)	4 (3.82, 0.89)	5 (4.84, 0.68)	5 (4.38, 1.04)	2 (1.79, 0.65)
RS	3 (3.31, 1.50)	2 (2.27, 1.26)	2 (2.07, 1.35)	3 (2.90, 1.63)	2.5 (2.68, 1.46)
GRS	4 (3.56, 1.25)	2 (2.31, 1.02)	2 (2.00, 1.14)	4 (3.26, 1.60)	3 (2.75, 1.22)

	double-object images				
Model	Grammar	Main Aspects	Correctness	Order	HumanLike
G	4 (3.80, 0.65)	5 (4.42, 0.97)	5 (4.69, 0.75)	5 (4.63, 0.79)	4 (3.77, 0.72)
GP	5 (4.44, 0.97)	5 (4.53, 0.81)	5 (4.81, 0.63)	5 (4.69, 0.81)	5 (4.43, 0.90)
RS	4 (3.39, 1.24)	2 (2.50, 1.25)	2 (2.20, 1.14)	2 (2.27, 1.26)	3 (2.93, 1.45)
GRS	3 (3.00, 1.41)	3 (3.14, 1.24)	2.5 (2.71, 1.32)	3 (2.93, 1.40)	3 (2.69, 1.52)
GPRS	3 (2.70, 1.32)	3 (2.87, 1.13)	2 (2.42, 1.16)	2 (2.45, 1.31)	2.5 (2.38, 1.31)

10 Conclusion and Future Work

This paper investigated the use of object labels and prepositions as keywords in a web-retrieval-based image caption generator. By employing object detection technology combined with a preposition prediction module, keywords were extracted in the form of object class labels and prepositions. The proposed retrieval approach is independent of any purposely human-annotated image datasets. Images were described by extracting sentences found in websites, featuring visually similar images to the query image. The search is aided with the use of the generated keywords. This approach was particularly effective when describing single-object images, and especially so when extracting sentences from stock photography websites.

Despite the retrieval of relevant descriptions for both single and double-object images, object labels connected with spatial prepositions obtained better accuracies when describing double-object images. Although Google's Search By Image was enhanced by the replacement of its predicted image annotations with object labels, further work in using a wider variety of keywords such as verbs can be carried out to improve the results. It is also worth studying whether linguistic parsing can be used to assess the quality of sentences during the caption extraction phase to increase the likelihood of choosing better sentences.

References

Ahmet Aker and Robert Gaizauskas. 2010. Generating image descriptions using dependency relational patterns. In *Proceedings of the 48th Annual Meeting of the Association for Computational Linguistics*, pages 1250–1258, Uppsala, Sweden, July. Association for Computational Linguistics.

Raffaella Bernardi, Ruket Cakici, Desmond Elliott, Aykut Erdem, Erkut Erdem, Nazli Ikizler-Cinbis, Frank Keller, Adrian Muscat, and Barbara Plank. 2016. Automatic description generation from images: A survey of models, datasets, and evaluation measures. *Journal of Artificial Intelligence Research*, 55(1):409–442, January.

Xinlei Chen and Lawrence Zitnick. 2015. Mind's eye: A recurrent visual representation for image caption generation. In *IEEE Conference on Computer Vision and Pattern Recognition, CVPR 2015, Boston, MA, USA, June 7-12, 2015*, pages 2422–2431.

Michael Denkowski and Alon Lavie. 2014. Meteor universal: Language specific translation evaluation for any target language. In *Proceedings of the Ninth Workshop on Statistical Machine Translation*, pages 376–380, Baltimore, Maryland, USA, June. Association for Computational Linguistics.

Jeff Donahue, Lisa Anne Hendricks, Sergio Guadarrama, Marcus Rohrbach, Subhashini Venugopalan, Trevor Darrell, and Kate Saenko. 2015. Long-term recurrent convolutional networks for visual recognition and description. In *IEEE Conference on Computer Vision and Pattern Recognition, CVPR 2015, Boston, MA, USA, June 7-12, 2015*, pages 2625–2634.

Hao Fang, Saurabh Gupta, Forrest N. Iandola, Rupesh Kumar Srivastava, Li Deng, Piotr Dollár, Jianfeng Gao, Xiaodong He, Margaret Mitchell, John C. Platt, Lawrence Zitnick, and Geoffrey Zweig. 2015. From captions to visual concepts and back. In *IEEE Conference on Computer Vision and Pattern Recognition, CVPR 2015, Boston, MA, USA, June 7-12, 2015*, pages 1473–1482.

Ali Farhadi, Mohsen Hejrati, Mohammad Amin Sadeghi, Peter Young, Cyrus Rashtchian, Julia Hockenmaier, and David Forsyth. 2010. Every picture tells a story: Generating sentences from images. In *Proceedings of the 11th European Conference on Computer Vision: Part IV*, ECCV'10, pages 15–29, Heraklion, Crete, Greece. Springer-Verlag.

Yansong Feng and Mirella Lapata. 2010. How many words is a picture worth? automatic caption generation for news images. In *Proceedings of the 48th Annual Meeting of the Association for Computational Linguistics*, pages 1239–1249, Uppsala, Sweden, July. Association for Computational Linguistics.

Ankush Gupta, Yashaswi Verma, and C. V. Jawahar. 2012. Choosing linguistics over vision to describe images. In *Proceedings of the Twenty-Sixth AAAI Conference on Artificial Intelligence*, AAAI'12, pages 606–612, Toronto, Ontario, Canada. AAAI Press.

Andrej Karpathy and Fei-Fei Li. 2015. Deep visual-semantic alignments for generating image descriptions. In *IEEE Conference on Computer Vision and Pattern Recognition, CVPR 2015, Boston, MA, USA, June 7-12, 2015*, pages 3128–3137.

Ryan Kiros, Ruslan Salakhutdinov, and Richard S. Zemel. 2014. Unifying visual-semantic embeddings with multimodal neural language models. *CoRR*, abs/1411.2539.

Christian Kohlschütter, Peter Fankhauser, and Wolfgang Nejdl. 2010. Boilerplate detection using shallow text features. In *Proceedings of the Third ACM International Conference on Web Search and Data Mining*, WSDM '10, pages 441–450, New York, NY, USA. ACM.

Girish Kulkarni, Visruth Premraj, Vicente Ordonez, Sagnik Dhar, Siming Li, Yejin Choi, Alexander C. Berg, and Tamara L. Berg. 2011. Baby talk: Understanding and generating simple image descriptions. In *Proceedings of the 2011 IEEE Conference on Computer Vision and Pattern Recognition*, CVPR '11, pages 1601–1608, Washington, DC, USA. IEEE Computer Society.

Siming Li, Girish Kulkarni, Tamara L. Berg, Alexander C. Berg, and Yejin Choi. 2011. Composing simple image descriptions using web-scale n-grams. In *Proceedings of the Fifteenth Conference on Computational Natural Language Learning*, pages 220–228, Portland, Oregon, USA, June. Association for Computational Linguistics.

Chin-Yew Lin and Eduard Hovy. 2003. Automatic evaluation of summaries using n-gram co-occurrence statistics. In *Proceedings of the 2003 Conference of the North American Chapter of the Association for Computational Linguistics on Human Language Technology - Volume 1*, NAACL '03, pages 71–78, Edmonton, Canada. Association for Computational Linguistics.

Tsung-Yi Lin, Michael Maire, Serge Belongie, James Hays, Pietro Perona, Deva Ramanan, Piotr Dollár, and Lawrence Zitnick. 2014. Microsoft COCO: Common objects in context. In David Fleet, Tomas Pajdla, Bernt Schiele, and Tinne Tuytelaars, editors, *Computer Vision – ECCV 2014: 13th European Conference, Zurich, Switzerland, September 6-12, 2014, Proceedings, Part V*, pages 740–755. Springer International Publishing, Cham.

Rebecca Mason and Eugene Charniak. 2014. Nonparametric method for data-driven image captioning. In *Proceedings of the 52nd Annual Meeting of the Association for Computational Linguistics (Volume 2: Short Papers)*, pages 592–598, Baltimore, Maryland, June. Association for Computational Linguistics.

Tomas Mikolov, Ilya Sutskever, Kai Chen, Greg Corrado, and Jeffrey Dean. 2013. Distributed representations of words and phrases and their compositionality. In *Proceedings of the 26th International Conference on Neural Information Processing Systems*, NIPS'13, pages 3111–3119, Lake Tahoe, Nevada. Curran Associates Inc.

Margaret Mitchell, Xufeng Han, Jesse Dodge, Alyssa Mensch, Amit Goyal, Alex Berg, Kota Yamaguchi, Tamara Berg, Karl Stratos, and Hal Daumé III. 2012. Midge: Generating image descriptions from computer vision detections. In *Proceedings of the 13th Conference of the European Chapter of the Association for Computational Linguistics*, EACL '12, pages 747–756, Avignon, France. Association for Computational Linguistics.

Adrian Muscat and Anja Belz. 2015. Generating descriptions of spatial relations between objects in images. In *Proceedings of the 15th European Workshop on Natural Language Generation (ENLG)*, pages 100–104, Brighton, UK, September. Association for Computational Linguistics.

Vicente Ordonez, Girish Kulkarni, and Tamara L Berg. 2011. Im2text: Describing images using 1 million captioned photographs. In *Proceedings of the 24th International Conference on Neural Information Processing Systems*, NIPS'11, pages 1143–1151, Granada, Spain. Curran Associates Inc.

Vicente Ordonez, Xufeng Han, Polina Kuznetsova, Girish Kulkarni, Margaret Mitchell, Kota Yamaguchi, Karl Stratos, Amit Goyal, Jesse Dodge, Alyssa Mensch, Hal Daumé III, Alexander C. Berg, Yejin Choi, and Tamara L. Berg. 2016. Large scale retrieval and generation of image descriptions. *Int. J. Comput. Vision*, 119(1):46–59, August.

Kishore Papineni, Salim Roukos, Todd Ward, and Wei-Jing Zhu. 2002. Bleu: a method for automatic evaluation of machine translation. In *Proceedings of 40th Annual Meeting of the Association for Computational Linguistics*, pages 311–318, Philadelphia, Pennsylvania, USA, July. Association for Computational Linguistics.

Arnau Ramisa, Josiah Wang, Ying Lu, Emmanuel Dellandrea, Francesc Moreno-Noguer, and Robert Gaizauskas. 2015. Combining geometric, textual and visual features for predicting prepositions in image descriptions. In *Proceedings of the 2015 Conference on Empirical Methods in Natural Language Processing*, pages 214–220, Lisbon, Portugal, September. Association for Computational Linguistics.

Shaoqing Ren, Kaiming He, Ross Girshick, and Jian Sun. 2015. Faster r-cnn: Towards real-time object detection with region proposal networks. In *Proceedings of the 28th International Conference on Neural Information Processing Systems*, NIPS'15, pages 91–99, Montreal, Canada. MIT Press.

Karen Simonyan and Andrew Zisserman. 2014. Very deep convolutional networks for large-scale image recognition. *CoRR*, abs/1409.1556.

Richard Socher, Andrej Karpathy, Quoc Le, Christopher Manning, and Andrew Ng. 2014. Grounded compositional semantics for finding and describing images with sentences. *Transactions of the Association for Computational Linguistics*, 2:207–218.

Ramakrishna Vedantam, Lawrence Zitnick, and Devi Parikh. 2015. Cider: Consensus-based image description evaluation. In *IEEE Conference on Computer Vision and Pattern Recognition, CVPR 2015, Boston, MA, USA, June 7-12, 2015*, pages 4566–4575.

Semih Yagcioglu, Erkut Erdem, Aykut Erdem, and Ruket Cakici. 2015. A distributed representation based query expansion approach for image captioning. In *Proceedings of the 53rd Annual Meeting of the Association for Computational Linguistics and the 7th International Joint Conference on Natural Language Processing (Volume 2: Short Papers)*, pages 106–111, Beijing, China, July. Association for Computational Linguistics.

Yezhou Yang, Ching Lik Teo, Hal Daumé III, and Yiannis Aloimonos. 2011. Corpus-guided sentence generation of natural images. In *Proceedings of the Conference on Empirical Methods in Natural Language Processing*, EMNLP '11, pages 444–454, Edinburgh, United Kingdom. Association for Computational Linguistics.

Learning to Recognize Animals by Watching Documentaries: Using Subtitles as Weak Supervision

Aparna Nurani Venkitasubramanian[1], **Tinne Tuytelaars**[2], **and Marie-Francine Moens**[1]

[1]KU Leuven, Computer Science Department, Belgium
[2]KU Leuven, ESAT-PSI, IMEC, Belgium
{firstname.lastname}@kuleuven.be

Abstract

We investigate animal recognition models learned from wildlife video documentaries by using the weak supervision of the textual subtitles. This is a challenging setting, since i) the animals occur in their natural habitat and are often largely occluded and ii) subtitles are to a great degree complementary to the visual content, providing a very weak supervisory signal. This is in contrast to most work on integrated vision and language in the literature, where textual descriptions are tightly linked to the image content, and often generated in a curated fashion for the task at hand. We investigate different image representations and models, in particular a support vector machine on top of activations of a pretrained convolutional neural network, as well as a Naive Bayes framework on a *'bag-of-activations'* image representation, where each element of the bag is considered separately. This representation allows key components in the image to be isolated, in spite of vastly varying backgrounds and image clutter, without an object detection or image segmentation step. The methods are evaluated based on how well they transfer to unseen camera-trap images captured across diverse topographical regions under different environmental conditions and illumination settings, involving a large domain shift.

1 Introduction

It is estimated[1] that video traffic will be 82 percent of all global Internet traffic by 2020. The ubiquitousness of video on the web demands indexing tools that facilitate fast and easy access to relevant content. Traditionally, video search has been based on user-tags. However, in the recent past, research activities have been directed at automatic indexing of videos based on the content. Contributing to this goal of automatic video indexing, we focus on the problem of wildlife recognition in nature documentaries with subtitles.

This setup is challenging from at least two perspectives: first, from the point of view of the *content*, and second, due to the *nature of video documentaries*. As far as the *content* is concerned, we are dealing with animals shot in their natural habitat. The problem of identifying animals in videos, especially those shot in the natural habitat presents several challenges. Firstly, animals are among the most difficult objects to recognize in images and videos, mainly due to their deformable bodies that often self occlude and the large variation they pose in appearance and depiction (Afkham et al., 2008; Berg and Forsyth, 2006). Further, in the natural habitat, there are challenges due to camouflage and occlusion by flora. Moreover, unlike faces or cuboidal objects such as furniture, we do not have accurate detectors that can localize the animal in a frame. State-of-the-art object proposal methods such as (Girshick et al., 2014; Ren et al., 2015) yield an unacceptably low level of either recall or precision. The absence of detectors necessitates other mechanisms that allow segregation of the components of the image.

The *nature of video documentaries* presents yet another challenge. Typically, in video documentaries such as ours, the subtitles are not parallel, but complementary to the visuals (See Fig. 1). This is in contrast to most work on integrated vision and language in the literature, where textual descriptions are tightly linked to the image content. This means we do not have examples that

[1]http://www.cisco.com/c/en/us/solutions/collateral/service-provider/visual-networking-index-vni/complete-white-paper-c11-481360.html

Proceedings of the 6th Workshop on Vision and Language, pages 21–30,
Valencia, Spain, April 4, 2017.

In the rivers and lakes of Africa, lives an animal which has a reputation for being the most unpredictable and dangerous of all.
Even **crocodiles** are wary.
The **hippopotamus**.

Figure 1: A set of frames together with the corresponding subtitles: The frames show hippos, while the subtitles mention both hippo and crocodile.

can reliably tie together textual and visual entities.

In this work, we study image representations and models that cope with the above challenges. These include a support vector machine on top of activations of a pretrained convolutional neural network, and a Naive Bayes framework on a *'bag-of-activations'* image representation, where each element of the bag is considered separately. While the former utilizes a *global representation* denoted by the feature vector comprising CNN activations, the latter works on per dimension basis, allowing key components in the image to be isolated, in spite of largely varying backgrounds and image clutter, without an object detection or image segmentation step. We experiment with both continuous and discretized variants of the *'bag-of-activations'* representation. In particular, *we investigate image representations and weakly supervised animal recognition models that can be learned without the need for bounding boxes, or curated data comprising manually annotated training examples.*

The rest of this paper is organized as follows: Section 2 presents the background and related work. Section 3 provides the problem definition. Section 4 describes the image representations and animal recognition models based on CNN activations. Section 5 discusses the experiments and results. Finally, Section 6 provides the conclusions.

2 Related Work

Identifying animals is a well-studied topic (Afkham et al., 2008; Berg and Forsyth, 2006; Schmid, 2001; Ramanan et al., 2006). Recent works such as (Hariharan and Girshick, 2016) and (Gomez and Salazar, 2016) advance us further and provide better insight into the problem. However, these methods are not applicable in our setting since they require extensive training data. It is important to note that in this setup, we lack sufficient reliable training data making neural network-based training impractical.

Apart from these works that focus specifically on animals, there is a large literature on generic object detection. These methods are often evaluated on the Pascal VOC challenge dataset (Everingham et al., 2012) which includes classes of animals such as cats, dogs, cows and horses, among other things. There are also datasets that focus on animals such as Caltech UCSD Birds (Wah et al., 2011) and Stanford Dogs (Khosla et al., 2011). Additionally, the FishClef and BirdClef challenges which are part of LifeClef (Joly et al., 2015) provide an arena for identification of species of fish and birds respectively. Most of these datasets are, however, object-centered and in that sense easier than the 'in-the-wild' setting we are dealing with.

The problem of aligning animals from videos with their mentions in subtitles has been studied in (Dusart et al., 2013) and (Venkitasubramanian et al., 2016). The former relies on hand-annotated bounding boxes to localize the animals in a frame, which are difficult to acquire. The latter relies on training animal classifiers on labeled external data such as ImageNet (Deng et al., 2009), and has the issue that not all classes of objects can be learned from an external dataset, for instance, rare species of animals may not be found on ImageNet.

Recently, there has been considerable interest in sentence/caption generation from images as well as natural language based object detection, e.g. (Karpathy and Fei-Fei, 2014; Fang et al., 2014; Guadarrama et al., 2013; Kazemzadeh et al., 2014). These approaches typically rely on text snippets that accurately describe the content of the images or videos. However, in our context, the subtitles and the visuals are not parallel, but complementary. For example, often a few animals are mentioned in the text, while the connected frame only shows one of them. The connection between the vision and the text is therefore much weaker. Additionally, in our setup, we have too few data to train similar models. As a result, these approaches are not directly applicable to our setting. In this paper, we explore weakly-supervised models that can deal with the complementarity or the 'non-parallelism' of the visual and textual modalities.

There has also been some work on alignment across modalities for recognizing people (Pham et al., 2010, 2011; Guillaumin et al., 2008). These approaches rely on the use of a face-detector. While there are face detectors available with reasonable accuracy, there are no such detectors that allow localizing animals. The absence of the bounding boxes complicates the problem in many ways. A notable endeavor in this domain is that of (Everingham et al., 2006) where dialogue transcripts and other supervisory information (such as lip movements or clothing) are used in addition to subtitles and face detectors. In our context, since the subjects of our videos involve animals, cues such as lip movements or clothing are not relevant.

In this paper, we investigate image representations and multi-modal animal recognition models that can cope with a) complementarity of vision and language, b) lack of bounding boxes and c) lack of labeled external data, and can transfer to a different unseen domain, shot under very different conditions.

3 Task definition

We have a wildlife documentary with subtitles. On the visual side, we derive key frames $\mathbf{F} = \{f_1, f_2 \dots f_q\}$ from which we extract visual features with a suitable representation $\mathbf{A} = \{\mathbf{a_1}, \mathbf{a_2} \dots \mathbf{a_q}\}$. Assume each feature vector has D dimensions. On the textual side, from the subtitles, we identify the $unique$ animal mentions or animal names $\mathbf{N} = \{n_1, n_2 \dots n_p\}$, using a list of animal names derived from WordNet (Miller, 1995) as in (Dusart et al., 2013).

Using the setup of (Venkitasubramanian et al., 2016), we associate every frame $f_i, 1 \leq i \leq q$, with a set $\mathbb{N}_i \subset \mathbf{N}$ of possible animal names derived from 5 subtitles to the left and right of the frame. The set $\mathbb{N}_i$ refers to the set of unique animal names derived from their mentions and coreferences in the subtitles[2]. It is possible that the frame has some or all or none of the animals in $\mathbb{N}_i$. Corresponding to every name $n_l \in \mathbb{N}_i$, we have a binary label y_l indicating the presence or absence of n_l. Our objective is to find the most likely value of y_l corresponding to name $n_l \in \mathbb{N}_i$ for every frame f_i.

4 Image Representations Based on CNN Activations

A popular choice of visual features for object recognition is the activations of the penultimate layer of a pretrained Convolutional Neural Network. In this work, we use the VGG CNN-M-128 architecture[3] of (Chatfield et al., 2014), which is trained on 1,000 object categories from ImageNet (Deng et al., 2009) with roughly 1.2M training images. Within this realm, we explore two perspectives on the real-valued feature vector: (i) a *global representation* where each feature vector is treated as one entity, and (ii) a *bag-of-activations* representation, where each element of the bag is considered separately.

The **global representation** is by far the most commonly used (Sharif Razavian et al., 2014) and fits well with a linear Support Vector Machine (SVM) classifier. For the task of object recognition, the linear SVM is typically used with the L_2 norm, and has the following objective function

$$\underset{\mathbf{w_l}}{\text{minimize}} \frac{1}{2}||\mathbf{w_l}||^2 + C\sum_i \max(1 - y_l \mathbf{w_l}^T \mathbf{a_i}, 0)$$

where $\mathbf{w_l}$ denotes the set of weights to be learned for the label y_l corresponding to name n_l, and C denotes the cost[4]. In a weakly supervised setting, these weights are learned based on the

[2]There remains a small percentage (2.35%) of animals not mentioned in the nearby subtitles. These will be left undetected.

[3]This model yielded 128 features.

[4]We used the Liblinear (Fan et al., 2008) toolkit, with the default setting of 1 for the cost C.

weakly associated (hence noisy) frame-name pairs $< \mathbf{a_i}, n_l >$ for all $n_l \in \mathbb{N}_i$.

An alternative to this *global representation* is a **bag-of-activations** representation, where each feature dimension is treated in isolation. Li et al. (2014) have shown that the CNN activations have two interesting properties: firstly, they can be treated independently along the dimensions and second, they preserve their essence even after binarization. We exploit the first property and use it in a naive Bayes framework. The idea of treating each element of the CNN representation individually rather than using the full feature vector in a high-dimensional space is crucial: *It brings robustness to image clutter and changing backgrounds, and helps in learning from few examples.*

$$p(y_l|\mathbf{a_i}) = \frac{p(y_l)\prod_{v=1}^{D} p(a_{iv}|y_l)}{Z_l} \qquad (1)$$

Z_l is a normalization constant for the name n_l, given by

$$Z_l = p(y_l)\prod_{v=1}^{D} p(a_{iv}|y_l) + p(\overline{y_l})\prod_{v=1}^{D} p(a_{iv}|\overline{y_l}) \quad (2)$$

where $\overline{y_l} = 0$ if $y_l = 1$ and vice versa. $p(y_l)$ is the prior which we assume to be uninformative for simplicity. So, $p(y_l = 0) = p(y_l = 1)$.

Then, using Eq. 2, Eq. 1 can be written as follows:

$$p(y_l|\mathbf{a_i}) = \frac{\prod_{v=1}^{D} p(a_{iv}|y_l)}{\prod_{v=1}^{D} p(a_{iv}|y_l) + \prod_{v=1}^{D} p(a_{iv}|\overline{y_l})} \quad (3)$$

The second interesting property of the CNN activations is that they preserve their essence even after binarization. We investigate this further and show that not only binarization but also **discretization** of the feature vector into a larger number of bins is useful. In particular, we propose to discretize the feature vector into B bins along each dimension[5]. In this paper, we experiment with two approaches for binning the feature vector - (i) equal width and (ii) equal frequency. The equal width approach ensures that all the bins are of the same size. For example, if we are interested in 2 equal width bins, we could look at the feature vector along a dimension and set the threshold midway between the minimum and maximum values of that dimension. The values that are less than the threshold could be set to 0, while the rest are set to 1. In equal frequency binning, the threshold is set such that the number of elements in each bin is roughly the same.

This discretization is similar to the vector quantization of SIFT descriptors to obtain Bag of Visual Words (BoVW). But, while BoVW has the issue that the discretization errors can have a significant negative impact, with CNN features, *there are no strong discretization artifacts*. In fact, Li et al. (2014) have shown that retaining just the values of the largest k dimensions (or even setting the values of the largest k dimensions to 1 and the rest to 0) is sufficient to capture the essence of the image.

Discretizing the feature space allows us to replace the feature a_{iv} by the corresponding bin β_v.

$$p(a_{iv}|y_l) = p(\beta_v|y_l) \qquad (4)$$

where $\beta_v \in \{0, 1 \ldots B\}$ is the bin to which a_{iv} belongs.

Eq. 3 can then be rewritten as

$$p(y_l|\mathbf{a_i}) = \frac{\prod_{v=1}^{D} p(\beta_v|y_l)}{\prod_{v=1}^{D} p(\beta_v|y_l) + \prod_{v=1}^{D} p(\beta_v|\overline{y_l})} \quad (5)$$

To compute the conditional probabilities $p(\beta_v|y_l)$ of the bin β_v given y_l, we rely on the noisy labels that can be obtained from the text. Basically we count the co-occurrence of label y_l corresponding to name $n_l \in \mathbb{N}_i$ with bin β_v relative to the total number of instances where y_l occurs in our dataset.

$$p(\beta_v|y_l) = \frac{freq(\beta_v, y_l)}{freq(y_l)} \qquad (6)$$

5 Experiments and Results

The dataset used in our experiments is that of (Dusart et al., 2013). This is a wildlife documentary named 'Great Wildlife Moments'[6] with subtitles from the BBC. This is an interlaced video with a duration of 108 minutes at a frame rate of 25 frames per second, and the frame resolution is 720x576 pixels. The video consists of 28 chapters and all the chapters except the ones containing just one animal are evaluated. This leaves us with chapters 14 to 28. Applying shot cut detection (Hellier et al., 2012) on these chapters, we obtained 602 key frames. Of these, 302 frames had

[5]Discretization can also be applied to the *global representation* used by the SVM, but as shown in (Venkitasubramanian et al., 2016), it is particularly useful in conjunction with a naive Bayes classifier.

[6]https://en.wikipedia.org/wiki/Great_Wildlife_Moments

Method	Precision	Recall	F_1
SVM	80.43	12.71	21.96
Naive Bayes	20.23	71.48	31.54

Table 1: Results of using the *continuous features* and applying the weak labels of our dataset

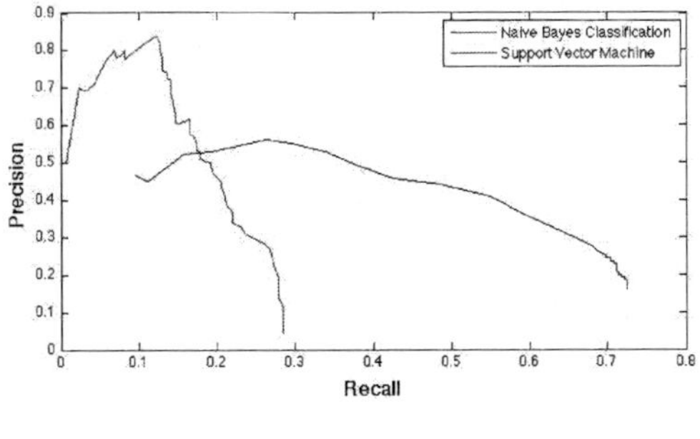

Figure 2: The precision-recall curves for the SVM and naive Bayes classifier shown in Table 1. Area under the curve is 0.1599 for the SVM and 0.3642 for naive Bayes.

no animal. The remaining 300 contained 365 animals in total. We run our algorithm on all the 602 key frames. There were 19 species of animals.

The animal labeling is evaluated in terms of precision, recall and F_1 computed over the entire dataset as follows:

$$\text{precision} = \frac{\text{number of labels correctly assigned}}{\text{total number of labels assigned}}$$

$$\text{recall} = \frac{\text{number of labels correctly assigned}}{\text{actual number of animal present}}$$

The evaluation covers two aspects:

1. How well do the representation and model learned using the weak labels of our dataset perform on the same dataset? (Section 5.1)

2. How well do the representation and model learned using the weak labels of our dataset transfer to an external dataset shot over diverse topographical regions under different environmental conditions and illumination settings? (Section 5.2)

5.1 Animal labeling on wildlife videos

Table 1 shows the performance of an SVM on the *global representation* and a naive Bayes classifier on the *bag of activations* using *continuous features*. In either case, name n_l is assigned to frame

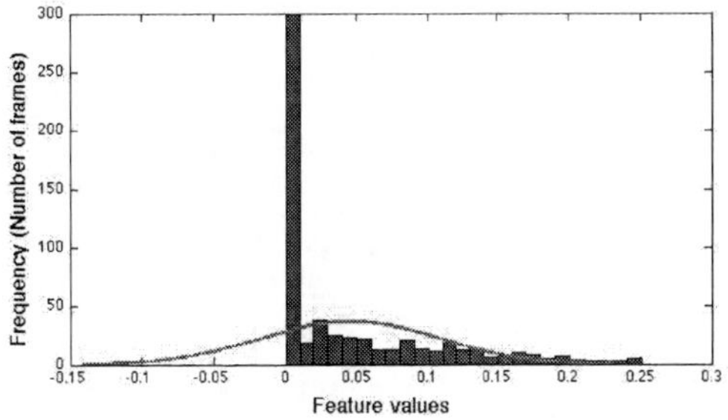

Figure 3: The distribution of the feature values along the first dimension: x-axis shows the range of feature values, y-axis shows the number of frames. The grey histogram shows the distribution of the feature values. The red curve is the normal distribution plotted using the mean and standard deviation along the first dimension, $\mathcal{N}(0.0454, 0.0622)$.

$\mathbf{a_i}$ if $p(y_l|\mathbf{a_i}) > p(\overline{y_l}|\mathbf{a_i})$, that is, the probability threshold for prediction was set at 0.5. For the naive Bayes classifier, a Gaussian distribution was used to model the continuous features along each dimension. While both models do not yield adequate performance, the naive Bayes certainly does far better compared to the SVM. In this setup involving limited reliable example pairs, *it is beneficial to treat each element of the CNN representation individually rather than using the full feature vector in a high-dimensional space*. Fig. 2 shows the precision-recall curves of the SVM and the naive Bayes classifier. The naive Bayes is clearly better in this setup, except in the low recall / high precision region.

Closer inspection reveals that the Gaussian distribution used in the Naive Bayes framework is not a good fit to the data (see Fig. 3 for one example feature dimension). Fig. 3 shows the normal distribution plotted using the mean and the standard deviation along the first dimension for the entire dataset (red curve: $\mathcal{N}(0.0454, 0.0622)$). This is superimposed on the histogram of the real-valued (undiscretized) feature vector (in grey). While there are certainly other distributions (such as Poisson or Binomial) that could be used to model the data, we show that the most commonly used Gaussian clearly does not fit the data. Rather than forcing the data to fit into some distribution, we turn to a discretized setting as it allows use of a simple non-parametric model.

Method	Precision	Recall	F_1
$B = 2$	46.43	91.55	61.61
$B = 3$	46.85	94.37	62.62
$B = 4$	47.03	92.96	62.46
$B = 5$	47.18	94.37	62.91
$B = 6$	47.88	95.31	63.74
$\boldsymbol{B = 7}$	47.69	96.71	**63.88**
$B = 8$	47.45	96.24	63.57
$B = 9$	47.00	95.77	63.06
$B = 20$	46.47	95.77	62.58
$log_2 l$-bins	47.47	96.71	63.68

Method	Precision	Recall	F_1
$B = 2$	48.04	92.02	63.12
$B = 3$	47.95	93.43	63.38
$B = 4$	46.99	95.31	62.95
$B = 5$	46.24	95.31	62.27
$B = 6$	45.56	96.24	61.84
$B = 7$	45.23	95.77	61.45
$B = 8$	44.93	95.77	61.17
$B = 9$	44.81	97.18	61.33
$B = 20$	43.51	97.65	60.20

Table 2: Results of using the *discretized features* (left: equal width discretization, right: equal frequency discretization) and applying the weak labels of our dataset

Next, we present the results of using the *discretized features*. Table 2 (left) shows the results of the animal labeling using equal width binning for different number of bins B. First, we use a fixed number of bins over every dimension. That is, along every dimension in the feature vector, the number of bins is set to a constant B. Note that irrespective of the number of bins, the performance has improved significantly. The precision has more than doubled, and the recall has improved by more than 20% absolute. *Contrary to expectations, the discretization has actually improved the classification.* These findings are consistent with those of Dougherty et al. (Dougherty et al., 1995). Overall, we see that these results are significantly better than all the baselines in Table 1. In addition to the discretization, the key aspects of this method are the use of naive Bayes classifier and the idea of treating each element of the CNN representation separately rather than using the full feature vector in a high-dimensional space. These bring robustness to image clutter and changing backgrounds, and help in learning from few examples.

Next, looking at the F_1 measures for different values of B, we see that the best results are obtained when $B = 7$. In addition to fixing the number of bins along every dimension, we used a heuristic to set a variable number of bins for each dimension. Using the heuristic in S-Plus histogram algorithm of Spector (Spector, 1994), we set the number of bins along each dimension to $log_2 l$, where l is the number of unique values in that dimension. Using this heuristic, different dimensions had different number of bins. We observed that of the 128 dimensions, 12 had 7 bins, while the rest had 8 bins. This explains why we have the best results in the range $B = 7$ and $B = 8$.

Table 2 (right) shows the results of the animal labeling using equal frequency binning for different number of bins B. Here, since we are dealing with sparse matrices, we have to ensure that all zero-valued entries along a dimension should belong to the same bin. The results in table 2 incorporate this correction. As with the equal-width case, we obtain significant improvements over the naive Bayes classifier with continuous features.

Fig. 4 shows some of the sample outputs of our system. Note that our method is capable of identifying multiple species in the same frame, as well as detecting frames that do not contain any animal.

5.2 Transfer to camera-trap images

The second aspect of the evaluation is to measure how well the representations and models transfer to external data from an entirely different setup. To evaluate this, we use the Snapshot Serengeti (Swanson et al., 2015) dataset, which consists of camera-trap (remote, automatic cameras) images covering wildlife in Savanna. We learn animal recognition models using the weak labels of our dataset and apply them to the Snapshot Serengeti (Swanson et al., 2015) dataset. It is important to note that the pictures of this Serengeti dataset are captured automatically, in very different scenes, under various illumination conditions. This causes a huge *domain shift*. The Serengeti dataset covers 40 mammalian species, of which three (Lion, Zebra and Hippopotamus) also appear in our dataset. We choose 500 random images[7] each of Lion and

[7] shot between 6:00 am and 6:00 pm

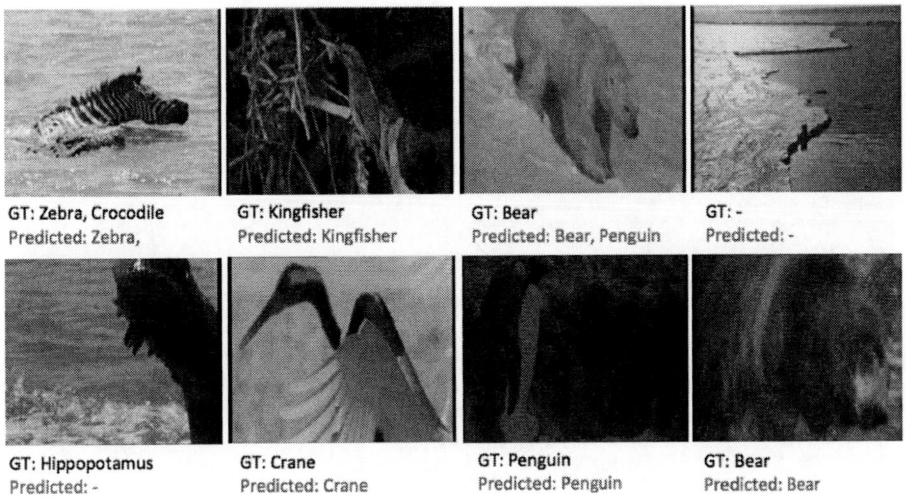

Figure 4: Some sample outputs from our system. 'GT' indicates ground truth, 'Predicted' indicates the predictions of the system.

Zebra, and all 37 images available for the Hippopotamus class. This set forms the target data on which the animal recognition models will be tested. Fig. 5 shows some of the sample images from this dataset.

Table 3 shows the performance of the animal recognition models learned using our data, applied on the target dataset. The first baseline is simply based on the probabilities output by the CNN pretrained on ImageNet. We used the same architecture (CNN-M-128) that was used for feature extraction. When the output probability for a certain class was >0.5, we concluded that the system predicted that class. Of course, multiple classes could be predicted for each key frame. Although some of the classes predicted covered 'lake side', 'hay' etc. which were not explicitly labeled in our setup, there were a lot of animals incorrectly predicted (which did not belong to our dataset of 19 animals). These included elephant, panther, camel, dugong. We filtered the outputs to just retain the 19 classes that were seen in our dataset. This increased the precision by a large margin (second row in the table). Next, we retained only the three classes that were common to our dataset and Serengeti dataset. While this gave a perfect precision, the recall stands low at approx. 20% in all the three cases above.

Next, we train an SVM (on the continuous features) on all the 19 classes of our dataset, using the weak association of the subtitles and applied them to Serengeti (Swanson et al., 2015) dataset (Second block on table 3). Note that the performance is low compared to ImageNet cases in the first block. *The model learned by the SVM on our dataset does not compare well with that of ImageNet, which was trained on several thousands of zebra, hippos and lions.* As with the previous block, filtering to the 3 relevant classes increases the precision by a large margin, while the recall stays the same. When we used the ground truth labels instead of the weak labels (which basically indicate if a frame could have some animal), we have a perfect precision, but the recall is even lower. By capturing elements in the background/environment which might be related to the animal, (e.g., a water body for the hippopotamus, or grasslands for the zebra), the training based on weak labels yields higher recall, albeit at the cost of precision.

The last block shows the performance using a naive Bayes, trained using both weak labels, and the ground truth. Again, we note that the precision is better with groundtruth labels, while the recall is lower. But in either case, there are remarkable improvements compared to the first and second blocks. *The idea of treating each element of the CNN representation individually rather than using the full feature vector in a high-dimensional space is crucial both for isolating the object(s) of interest from the clutter, and for learning with few examples.* The discretized naive Bayes does not perform better than the continuous naive Bayes in this case - the discretized features probably do not

Figure 5: Some sample images from the Snapshot Serengeti (Swanson et al., 2015) dataset, together with the descriptions that show the difficulty of the task. Green box indicates the animal was recognized correctly, while red indicates the animal was missed.

Method	Precision	Recall	F_1
CNN-M-128 (1000 classes)	21.98	20.38	21.15
CNN-M-128 (filtered to 19 classes of our dataset)	91.75	20.38	33.35
CNN-M-128 (filtered to 3 overlapping classes)	100	20.38	33.86
SVM continuous (on our 19 classes) - using weak labels	58.16	14.96	23.80
SVM continuous (on 3 overlapping classes) - using weak labels	86.34	14.96	25.50
SVM continuous (on 3 overlapping classes) - using GT	100	9.31	17.04
NBC continuous (on 3 overlapping classes) - using weak labels	49.03	90.53	63.61
NBC continuous (on 3 overlapping classes) - using GT	62.07	67.71	64.77
NBC discretized into $log_2 l$ bins (on 3 classes) - using weak labels	53.45	65.73	58.95

Table 3: Performance of the animal recognition models learned using our data, applied on images from Snapshot Serengeti (Swanson et al., 2015) dataset

transfer as well to the target domain. Nevertheless, it certainly outperforms the classifiers in the first two blocks, by a large margin.

6 Conclusions

In this paper, we investigate different image representations and models, including a support vector machine on top of activations of a pretrained convolutional neural network, as well as a Naive Bayes framework on a *bag-of-activations* image representation, where each element of the bag is considered separately. We show that the *bag-of-activations* representation allows key components in the image to be isolated, in spite of largely varying backgrounds and image clutter, and eliminates the need for an object detection or image segmentation step. *In contrast to most work on integrated vision and language that use curated data, the proposed approach deals with vision and language that are complementary.*

When the source and target are of the same domain, we also found that the discretization used with a multinomial Naive Bayes classifier yields much better performance compared to continuous features with a traditional Naive Bayes classifier - the precision is more than doubled and the recall is boosted by more than 20% absolute for the task of identifying animals on a challenging dataset of wildlife documentaries. Here, we have used unsupervised equal-width and equal-frequency binning of the features. In future, we wish to explore other (weakly) supervised techniques for discretization, and their transfer to other domains. The methods proposed here take us a step closer to automatic video recognition and indexing.

References

Heydar Maboudi Afkham, Alireza Tavakoli Targhi, Jan-Olof Eklundh, and Andrzej Pronobis. 2008. Joint visual vocabulary for animal classification. In *19th International Conference on Pattern Recognition*. IEEE, pages 1–4.

Tamara L. Berg and David A. Forsyth. 2006. Animals on the web. In *IEEE Computer Society Conference on Computer Vision and Pattern Recognition*. IEEE, volume 2, pages 1463–1470.

Ken Chatfield, Karen Simonyan, Andrea Vedaldi, and Andrew Zisserman. 2014. Return of the devil in the details: Delving deep into convolutional nets. *In Proceedings of the British Machine Vision Conference* .

Jia Deng, Wei Dong, Richard Socher, Li-Jia Li, Kai Li, and Li Fei-Fei. 2009. Imagenet: A large-scale hierarchical image database. In *IEEE Conference on Computer Vision and Pattern Recognition*. IEEE, pages 248–255.

James Dougherty, Kohavi Ron, and Sahami Mehran. 1995. Supervised and unsupervised discretization of continuous features. In *Proceedings of the twelfth international conference on Machine Learning*. San Francisco, CA: Morgan Kaufmann, volume 12, page 194–202.

Thibaut Dusart, Aparna Nurani Venkitasubramanian, and Marie-Francine Moens. 2013. Cross-modal alignment for wildlife recognition. In *Proceedings of the 2nd ACM International Workshop on Multimedia Analysis for Ecological Data*. ACM, pages 9–14.

Mark Everingham, Josef Sivic, and Andrew Zisserman. 2006. Hello! my name is... buffy"–automatic naming of characters in tv video. In *Proceedings of the British Machine Vision Conference*. volume 2, page 6.

Mark Everingham, Luc Van Gool, Cristopher K. I. Williams, John Winn, and Andrew Zisserman. 2012. The PASCAL Visual Object Classes Challenge 2012 (VOC2012) Results.

Rong-En Fan, Kai-Wei Chang, Cho-Jui Hsieh, Xiang-Rui Wang, and Chih-Jen Lin. 2008. Liblinear: A library for large linear classification. *Journal of Machine Learning Research* 9:1871–1874.

Hao Fang, Saurabh Gupta, Forrest Iandola, Rupesh Srivastava, Li Deng, Piotr Dollár, Jianfeng Gao, Xiaodong He, Margaret Mitchell, John Platt, et al. 2014. From captions to visual concepts and back. *arXiv preprint arXiv:1411.4952* .

Ross Girshick, Jeff Donahue, Trevor Darrell, and Jitendra Malik. 2014. Rich feature hierarchies for accurate object detection and semantic segmentation. In *Proceedings of the IEEE Conference on Computer Vision and Pattern Recognition*. pages 580–587.

Alexander Gomez and Augusto Salazar. 2016. Towards automatic wild animal monitoring: Identification of animal species in camera-trap images using very deep convolutional neural networks. *arXiv preprint arXiv:1603.06169* .

Sergio Guadarrama, Niveda Krishnamoorthy, Girish Malkarnenkar, Subhashini Venugopalan, Raymond Mooney, Trevor Darrell, and Kate Saenko. 2013. Youtube2text: Recognizing and describing arbitrary activities using semantic hierarchies and zero-shot recognition. In *IEEE International Conference on Computer Vision*. IEEE, pages 2712–2719.

Matthieu Guillaumin, Thomas Mensink, Jakob Verbeek, and Cordelia Schmid. 2008. Automatic face naming with caption-based supervision. In *IEEE Conference on Computer Vision and Pattern Recognition*. IEEE, pages 1–8.

Bharath Hariharan and Ross Girshick. 2016. Low-shot visual object recognition. *arXiv preprint arXiv:1606.02819* .

Pierre Hellier, Vincent Demoulin, Lionel Oisel, and Patrick Pérez. 2012. A contrario shot detection. In *19th IEEE International Conference on Image Processing*. IEEE, pages 3085–3088.

Alexis Joly, Hervé Goëau, Hervé Glotin, Concetto Spampinato, Pierre Bonnet, Willem-Pier Vellinga, Robert Planqué, Andreas Rauber, Simone Palazzo, Bob Fisher, et al. 2015. Lifeclef 2015: multimedia life species identification challenges. In *International Conference of the Cross-Language Evaluation Forum for European Languages*. Springer, pages 462–483.

Andrej Karpathy and Li Fei-Fei. 2014. Deep visual-semantic alignments for generating image descriptions. *arXiv preprint arXiv:1412.2306* .

Sahar Kazemzadeh, Vicente Ordonez, Mark Matten, and Tamara L. Berg. 2014. Referit game: Referring to objects in photographs of natural scenes. In *Proceedings of the Conference on Empirical Methods in Natural Language Processing*.

Aditya Khosla, Nityananda Jayadevaprakash, Bangpeng Yao, and Fei-fei Li. 2011. Novel dataset for fine-grained image categorization. In *First Workshop on Fine-Grained Visual Categorization, IEEE Computer Society Conference on Computer Vision and Pattern Recognition*. Citeseer.

Yao Li, Lingqiao Liu, Chunhua Shen, and Anton van den Hengel. 2014. Mid-level deep pattern mining. *arXiv preprint arXiv:1411.6382* .

George A. Miller. 1995. WordNet: A lexical database for English. *Communications of the ACM* 38:39–41.

Phi The Pham, Marie-Francine Moens, and Tinne Tuytelaars. 2010. Cross-media alignment of names and faces. *IEEE Transactions on Multimedia* 12(1):13–27.

Phi The Pham, Tinne Tuytelaars, and Marie-Francine Moens. 2011. Naming people in news videos with label propagation. *IEEE Multimedia* 18(3):44–55.

Deva Ramanan, David A Forsyth, and Kobus Barnard. 2006. Building models of animals from video. *IEEE Transactions on Pattern Analysis and Machine Intelligence,* 28(8):1319–1334.

Shaoqing Ren, Kaiming He, Ross Girshick, and Jian Sun. 2015. Faster R-CNN: Towards real-time object detection with region proposal networks. In *Advances in Neural Information Processing systems.* pages 91–99.

Cordelia Schmid. 2001. Constructing models for content-based image retrieval. In *Proceedings of the IEEE Computer Society Conference on Computer Vision and Pattern Recognition,.* IEEE, volume 2, pages II–39.

Ali Sharif Razavian, Hossein Azizpour, Josephine Sullivan, and Stefan Carlsson. 2014. CNN features off-the-shelf: an astounding baseline for recognition. In *Proceedings of the IEEE Conference on Computer Vision and Pattern Recognition Workshops.* pages 806–813.

Phil Spector. 1994. An introduction to S and S-PLUS. *Duxbury press: Wadsworth, Inc .*

Alexandra Swanson, Margaret Kosmala, Chris Lintott, Robert Simpson, Arfon Smith, and Craig Packer. 2015. Snapshot Serengeti, high-frequency annotated camera trap images of 40 mammalian species in an African savanna. *Scientific Data* 2:150026.

Aparna Nurani Venkitasubramanian, Tinne Tuytelaars, and Marie-Francine Moens. 2016. Wildlife recognition in nature documentaries with weak supervision from subtitles and external data. *Pattern Recognition Letters, Elsevier* 81:63–70.

Catherine Wah, Steve Branson, Peter Welinder, Pietro Perona, and Serge Belongie. 2011. The Caltech-UCSD birds-200-2011 dataset, Technical Report CNS-TR-2011-001, California Institute of Technology .

Human Evaluation of Multi-modal Neural Machine Translation: a Case Study on E-commerce Listing Titles

Iacer Calixto[1], **Daniel Stein**[2], **Evgeny Matusov**[2], **Sheila Castilho**[1] **and Andy Way**[1]

[1]ADAPT Centre, School of Computing, Dublin City University, Dublin, Ireland
[2]eBay Inc., Aachen, Germany
{iacer.calixto,sheila.castilho,andy.way}@adaptcentre.ie
{danstein,ematusov}@ebay.com

Abstract

In this paper, we study how humans perceive the use of images as an additional knowledge source to machine-translate user-generated product listings in an e-commerce company. We conduct a human evaluation where we assess how a multi-modal neural machine translation (NMT) model compares to two text-only approaches: a conventional state-of-the-art attention-based NMT and a phrase-based statistical machine translation (PBSMT) model. We evaluate translations obtained with different systems and also discuss the data set of user-generated product listings, which in our case comprises both product listings and associated images. We found that humans preferred translations obtained with a PBSMT system to both text-only and multi-modal NMT over 56% of the time. Nonetheless, human evaluators ranked translations from a multi-modal NMT model as better than those of a text-only NMT over 88% of the time, which suggests that images do help NMT in this use-case.

1 Introduction

In e-commerce, leveraging Machine Translation (MT) to make products accessible regardless of the customer's native language or country of origin is a very persuasive use-case. In this work, we study how humans perceive the machine translation of user-generated auction listings' titles as listed on the eBay main site[1]. Among the challenges for MT are the specialized language and grammar for listing titles, as well as a high percentage of user-generated content for non-business sellers, who are often not native speakers themselves. This is reflected on the data by means of extremely high trigram perplexities of product listings, which is in 4 digit numbers even for language models (LMs) trained on in-domain data, as we discuss in §3. This is not only a challenge for LMs but also for automatic evaluation metrics such as the n-gram precision-based BLEU metric (Papineni et al., 2002).

The majority of listings are accompanied by a product image, often (but not always) a user-generated shot. Moreover, images are known to bring useful complementary information to MT (Calixto et al., 2012; Hitschler et al., 2016; Huang et al., 2016; Calixto et al., 2017b). Therefore, in order to explore whether product images can benefit the machine translation of auction titles, we evaluate a multi-modal neural MT (NMT) system to eBay's production system, specifically a phrase-based statistical MT (PBSMT) one. We additionally train a text-only attention-based NMT baseline, so as to be able to measure eventual gains from the additional multi-modal data independently of the MT architecture.

According to a quantitative evaluation using a combination of four automatic MT evaluation metrics, a PBSMT system outperforms both text-only and multi-modal NMT models in the translation of product listings, contrary to recent findings (Bentivogli et al., 2016). We hypothesise that these automatic metrics were not created for the purpose of measuring the impact an image brings to an MT model, so we conduct a human evaluation of translations generated by three different systems: a PBSMT, a text-only attention-based NMT and a multi-modal NMT system. With that human evaluation we wish to see whether those findings corroborate the automatic scores or instead support results included in recent papers in the literature.

The remainder of the paper is structured as follows. In §2 we briefly describe the text-only and multi-modal MT models we evaluate in this work and in §3 the data sets we used, together with a discussion of interesting findings. In §4 we discuss how we structure our evaluation and in §5 we analyse and discuss our results. In §6 we discuss important related work and finally in §7 we draw conclusions and suggest avenues for future work.

2 MT Models evaluated in this work

We first introduce the two text-only baselines used in this work: a PBSMT model (§2.1) and a text-only attention-based NMT model (§2.2). We then briefly discuss the doubly-attentive multi-modal NMT model we use in our experiments (§2.3), which is comparable to the model evaluated by Calixto et al. (2016) and further detailed and analysed in Calixto et al. (2017a).

[1]http://www.ebay.com/

Proceedings of the 6th Workshop on Vision and Language, pages 31–37,
Valencia, Spain, April 4, 2017.

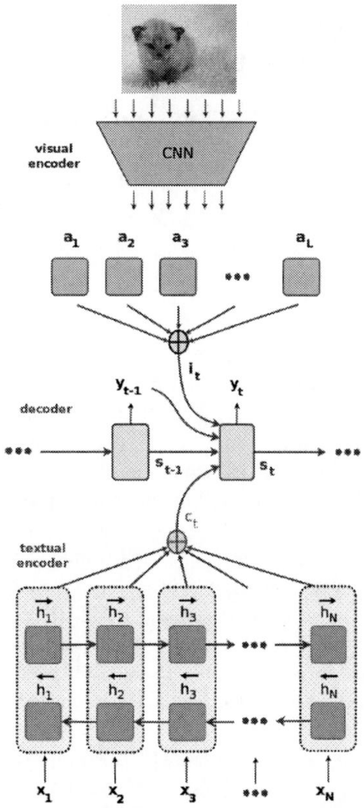

Figure 1: Decoder RNN with attention over source sentence and image features. This decoder learns to independently attend to image patches and source-language words when generating translations.

2.1 Statistical Machine Translation (SMT)

We use a PBSMT model where the language model (LM) is a 5–gram LM with modified Kneser-Ney smoothing (Kneser and Ney, 1995). We use minimum error rate training (Och, 2003) for tuning the model parameters using BLEU as the objective function.

2.2 Text-only NMT (NMT_t)

We use the attention-based NMT model introduced by Bahdanau et al. (2015) as our text-only NMT baseline. It is based on the encoder–decoder framework and it implements an attention mechanism over the source-sentence words $X = (x_1, x_2, \cdots, x_N)$, where $Y = (y_1, y_2, \cdots, y_M)$ is its target-language translation. A model is trained to maximise the log-likelihood of the target given the source.

The encoder is a bidirectional recurrent neural network (RNN) with GRU units (Cho et al., 2014). The annotation vector for a given source word x_i is the concatenation of forward and backward vectors $\boldsymbol{h}_i = [\overrightarrow{\boldsymbol{h}}_i; \overleftarrow{\boldsymbol{h}}_i]$ obtained with forward and backward RNNs, respectively, and $\text{C} = (\boldsymbol{h}_1, \boldsymbol{h}_2, \cdots, \boldsymbol{h}_N)$ is the set of source annotation vectors.

The decoder is also an RNN, more specifically a neural LM (Bengio et al., 2003) conditioned upon its past predictions via its previous hidden state $\boldsymbol{s}_{t-1}$ and the word emitted in the previous time step y_{t-1}, as well as the source sentence via an attention mechanism. The attention computes a context vector $\boldsymbol{c}_t$ for each time step t of the decoder where this vector is a weighted sum of the source annotation vectors C:

$$\boldsymbol{e}^{\text{src}}_{t,i} = (\boldsymbol{v}^{\text{src}}_a)^T \tanh(\boldsymbol{U}^{\text{src}}_a \boldsymbol{s}_{t-1} + \boldsymbol{W}^{\text{src}}_a \boldsymbol{h}_i), \quad (1)$$

$$\boldsymbol{\alpha}^{\text{src}}_{t,i} = \frac{\exp(\boldsymbol{e}^{\text{src}}_{t,i})}{\sum_{j=1}^{N} \exp(\boldsymbol{e}^{\text{src}}_{t,j})}, \quad (2)$$

$$\boldsymbol{c}_t = \sum_{i=1}^{N} \alpha^{\text{src}}_{t,i} \boldsymbol{h}_i, \quad (3)$$

where $\alpha^{\text{src}}_{t,i}$ is the normalised alignment matrix between each source annotation vector $\boldsymbol{h}_i$ and the word to be emitted at time step t, and $\boldsymbol{v}^{\text{src}}_a$, $\boldsymbol{U}^{\text{src}}_a$ and $\boldsymbol{W}^{\text{src}}_a$ are model parameters.

2.3 Multi-modal NMT (NMT_m)

We use a multi-modal NMT model similar to the one evaluated by Calixto et al. (2016) and further studied in Calixto et al. (2017a), illustrated in Figure 1. It can be seen as an expansion of the attentive NMT framework described in §2.2 with the addition of a *visual component* to incorporate local visual features.

We use a publicly available pre-trained Convolutional Neural Network (CNN), namely the 50-layer Residual Network (ResNet-50) of He et al. (2016) to extract convolutional image features $(\boldsymbol{a}_1, \cdots, \boldsymbol{a}_L)$ for all images in our dataset. These features are extracted from the `res4f` layer and consist of a 196 x 1024 dimensional matrix where each row, i.e. a 1024D vector, represents features from a specific area and so only encodes information about that specific area of the image.

The visual attention mechanism computes a context vector $\boldsymbol{i}_t$ for each time step t of the decoder similarly to the textual attention mechanism described in §2.2:

$$\boldsymbol{e}^{\text{img}}_{t,l} = (\boldsymbol{v}^{\text{img}}_a)^T \tanh(\boldsymbol{U}^{\text{img}}_a \boldsymbol{s}_{t-1} + \boldsymbol{W}^{\text{img}}_a \boldsymbol{a}_l), \quad (4)$$

$$\boldsymbol{\alpha}^{\text{img}}_{t,l} = \frac{\exp(\boldsymbol{e}^{\text{img}}_{t,l})}{\sum_{j=1}^{L} \exp(\boldsymbol{e}^{\text{img}}_{t,j})}, \quad (5)$$

$$\boldsymbol{i}_t = \sum_{l=1}^{L} \alpha^{\text{img}}_{t,l} \boldsymbol{a}_l, \quad (6)$$

where $\alpha^{\text{img}}_{t,l}$ is the normalised alignment matrix between each image annotation vector $\boldsymbol{a}_l$ and the word to be emitted at time step t, and $\boldsymbol{v}^{\text{img}}_a$, $\boldsymbol{U}^{\text{img}}_a$ and $\boldsymbol{W}^{\text{img}}_a$ are model parameters.

3 Data sets

We use the data set of product listings and images produced by eBay, henceforth referred to as eBay24k, which consists of 23,697 tuples of products each containing *(i)* a product listing in English, *(ii)* a product listing in German and *(iii)* a product image. In ~6k training tuples, the original user-generated product listing was given in English and was manually translated into German by in-house experts. The same holds for validation and test sets, which contain 480 and 444 triples, respectively. In the remaining training tuples (~18k), the original listing was given in German and manually translated into English. We also use the publicly available Multi30k dataset (Elliott et al., 2016), a multilingual expansion of the original Flickr30k (Young et al., 2014) with ~30k pictures from Flickr, each accompanied by one description in English and one human translation of the English description into German.

Although the curation of in-domain parallel product listings with an associated product image is costly and time-consuming, monolingual German listings with an image are far simpler to obtain. In order to increase the small amount of training data, we train the text-only model NMT_t on the German–English eBay24k and Multi30k data sets (without images) and back-translate 83,832 German in-domain product listings into English. We use the synthetic English, original German and original image as additional training tuples, henceforth eBay80k.

The translation of user-generated product titles raises particular challenges; they are often ungrammatical and can be difficult to interpret in isolation even by a native speaker of the language, as illustrated in Table 1. We note that the listings in both languages have many scattered keywords and/or phrases glued together, as well as few typos (e.g., English listing in the first example). Moreover, in the second example the product image has a white frame surrounding it. These are all complications that make the multi-modal MT of product listings a challenging task, where there are different difficulties derived from processing listings and images.

To further demonstrate these issues, we compute perplexity scores with LMs trained on one in-domain and one general-domain German corpus: the Multi30k (~ 29k sentences) and eBay's in-domain data (~ 99k sentences), respectively.[2] The LM trained on the Multi30k computes a perplexity of 25k on the eBay test set, and the LM trained on the in-domain eBay data produces a perplexity of 4.2k on the Multi30k test set. We note that the LM trained on eBay's in-domain data still computes a very high perplexity on eBay's test set (ppl = 1.8k). These perplexity scores indicate that *fluency* might not be a good metric to use in our study, i.e. we should not expect a fluent machine-translated output of a model trained on poorly fluent training data.

[2]These are 5-gram LMs trained with KenLM (Heafield et al., 2013) using modified Kneser-Ney smoothing on tokenized, lowercased data.

Image	Product Listing
	(en) apple macbook pro 13.3" laptop - dvd - rw drive / good screen / airport card keyboar (de) apple macbook pro laptop 13.3" - dvd - rw - laufwerk / gutes display / airport karte tastatur
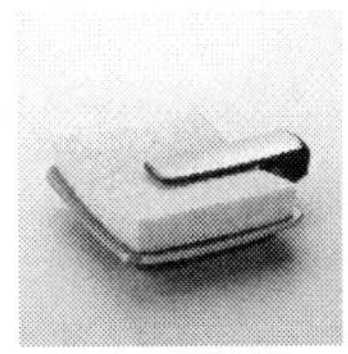	(en) modern napkin holder table top stainless steel weighted arm napkins paper towels (de) moderner tischserviettenhalter aus edelstahl mit beschwertem arm für servietten und papiertücher

Table 1: Examples of product listings accompanied by product images from the eBay test set.

Listing language	N	Difficulty listing only	Difficulty listing+image	Adequacy listing+image
English	20	2.50 ± 0.84	2.40 ± 0.84	2.45 ± 0.49
German	15	2.83 ± 0.75	**2.00** ± 0.50	2.39 ± 0.78

Table 2: Difficulty to understand product listings with and without images and adequacy of listings and images. N is the number of raters (Calixto et al., 2017b).

3.1 English and German product listings

Clearly, user-generated product listings are not very fluent in terms of grammar or even predictable word order. To better understand whether this has an impact on semantic intelligibility, Calixto et al. (2017b) have recently conducted experiments using eBay data to assess how challenging listings are to understand for a human reader. Specifically, they asked users how they perceive product listings with and without having the associated images available, under the hypothesis that images bring additional understanding to their corresponding listings.

In Table 2, we show results which suggest that the intelligibility of both the English and German product listings are perceived to be somewhere between "easy" and "neutral" when images are also available. It is notable that, in case of German, there is a statistically significant difference between the group who had access to the image and the product listing (M=2.00, SD=.50) and the group who only viewed the listing (M=2.83, ST=.30), where F(1,13) = 6.72, $p < 0.05$. Furthermore, humans find that product listings describe the associated image somewhere between "well" and "neutral" with no statistically significant differences between the adequacy of product listings and images in different languages (Calixto et al., 2017b).

Altogether, we have a strong indication that images can indeed help an MT model translate product listings, especially for translations into German.

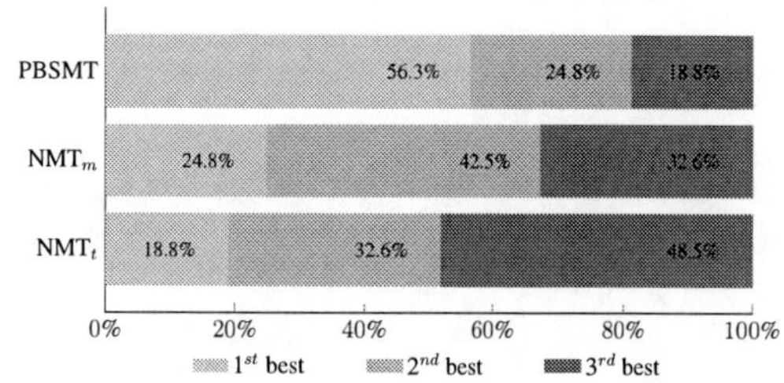

Figure 2: Models PBSMT, NMT_t and NMT_m ranked by humans from best to worst.

4 Experimental set-up

We use the eBay24k, the additional back-translated eBay80k and the Multi30k (Elliott et al., 2016) data sets to train all our models. In our experiments, we wish to contrast the human assessments of the adequacy of translations obtained with two text-only baselines, PBSMT and NMT_t, and one multi-modal model NMT_m, with scores computed with four automatic MT metrics: BLEU4 (Papineni et al., 2002), METEOR (Denkowski and Lavie, 2014), TER (Snover et al., 2006), and chrF3 (Popović, 2015).[3] We report statistical significance with approximate randomisation for the first three metrics using the MultEval tool (Clark et al., 2011).

For our qualitative human evaluation, we ask bilingual native German speakers:

1. to assess the *multi-modal adequacy* of translations (number of participants $N = 18$), described in §4.1;
2. to *rank* translations generated by different models from best to worst (number of participants $N = 18$), described in §4.2.

On average, our evaluators' consisted of 72% women and 28% men. They were recruited from employees at eBay Inc., Aachen, Germany, as well as the student and staff body of Dublin City University, Dublin, Ireland.

4.1 Adequacy

Humans are presented with an English product listing, a product image and a translation generated by one of the models (without knowing which model). They are then asked how much of the meaning of the source is also expressed in the translation, taking the product image into consideration. They must then select from a four-level Likert scale where the answers range from *1 – All of it* to *4 – None of it*.

4.2 Ranking

We present humans with a product image and three translations obtained from different models for a particular English product listing (without identifying the models) and ask them to rank translations from best to worst.

[3]We specifically compute character 6-gram F3.

5 Results

In Table 3, we contrast the human assessments of the adequacy of translations obtained with two text-only baselines, PBSMT and NMT_t, and one multi-modal model NMT_m, with scores obtained computing four MT automatic metrics.

Both models NMT_m and PBSMT improve on model NMT_t's translations according to the first three automatic metrics ($p < 0.01$), and we also observe improvements in chrF3. Although a one-way anova did not show any statistically significant differences in adequacy between NMT_m and NMT_t ($F(2, 18) = 1.29$, $p > 0.05$), human evaluators ranked NMT_m as better than NMT_t over 88% of the time, a strong indication that images do help neural MT and bring important information that the multi-modal model NMT_m can efficiently exploit.

If we compare models NMT_m and PBSMT, the latter outperforms the former according to BLEU, METEOR and chrF3, but they are practically equal according to TER. Additionally, the adequacy scores for both these models are, on average, the same according to scores computed over $N = 18$ different human assessments. Nonetheless, even though both models NMT_m and PBSMT are found to produce equally adequate output, translations obtained with PBSMT are ranked best by humans over 56.3% of the time, while translations obtained with the multi-modal model NMT_m are ranked best 24.8% of the time, as can be seen in Figure 2.

We stress that the multi-modal model NMT_m consistently outperforms the text-only model NMT_t, according to all four automatic metrics used in this work. Translations generated by model NMT_m contain many neologisms, possibly due to training these models using sub-word tokens rather than just words (Sennrich et al., 2016). Some examples are: "sammlerset", "garagenskateboard", "kampffaltschlocker", "schneidsattel" and "oberreceiver". We argue that this generative quality of the NMT models and the data sets evaluated in this work could have made translations more confusing for native German speakers to understand, therefore the preference for the SMT translations.[4]

We note that the pairwise inter-annotator agreement for the ranking task shows a *fair* agreement among the annotators ($\kappa = 0.30$), computed using Cohen's kappa coefficient (Cohen, 1960). For all the other evaluations, according to Landis and Koch (1977) the pairwise inter-annotator agreement can be interpreted as *slight* ($\kappa = 0.15$ for the multi-modal translation adequacy). The lower agreement score seems plausible since our annotators were crowdsourced and so had limited guidelines and less training for the tasks that would have been ideal.

[4]The SMT model was trained on words directly and therefore does not present these issues.

Model	BLEU4↑	METEOR↑	TER↓	chrF3↑	Adequacy↓
NMT_t	22.5	40.0	58.0	56.7	$2.71 \pm .48$
NMT_m	$25.1^{\dagger}$	$42.6^{\dagger}$	$\mathbf{55.5}^{\dagger}$	58.6	$\mathbf{2.36} \pm .47$
PBSMT	$\mathbf{27.4}^{\dagger\ddagger}$	$\mathbf{45.8}^{\dagger\ddagger}$	$\mathbf{55.4}^{\dagger}$	**61.6**	$\mathbf{2.36} \pm .47$

Table 3: Adequacy of translations and four automatic metrics on eBay's test set: BLEU, METEOR, TER and chrF3. For the first three metrics, results are significantly better than those of NMT_t (†) or NMT_m (‡) with $p < 0.01$.

6 Related work

Multi-modal MT has just recently been addressed by the MT community in a shared task (Specia et al., 2016), where many different groups proposed techniques for multi-modal translation using different combinations of NMT and SMT models (Caglayan et al., 2016; Calixto et al., 2016; Huang et al., 2016; Libovický et al., 2016; Shah et al., 2016). In the multi-modal translation task, participants are asked to train models to translate image descriptions from one natural language into another, while also taking the image itself into consideration. This effectively bridges the gap between two well-established tasks: image description generation (IDG) and MT.

There is an important body of research conducted in IDG. We highlight the work of Vinyals et al. (2015), who proposed an influential neural IDG model based on the sequence-to-sequence framework. They used global visual features to initialise an RNN LM decoder, used to generate the image descriptions in a target language, word by word. In contrast, Xu et al. (2015) were among the first to propose an attention-based model where a model learns to attend to specific areas of an image representation as it generates its description in natural language with a soft-attention mechanism. In their model, local visual features were used instead. In both cases, as well as in this work and in most of the state-of-the-art models in the field, models transferred learning from CNNs pre-trained for image classification on ImageNet (Russakovsky et al., 2015).

In NMT, Bahdanau et al. (2015) was the first to propose to use an attention mechanism in the decoder. Their decoder learns to attend to the relevant source-language words as it generates a sentence in the target language, again word by word. Since then, many authors have proposed different ways to incorporate attention into MT. Luong et al. (2015) proposed among other things a local attention mechanism that was less costly than the original global attention; Firat et al. (2016) proposed a model to translate from many source and into many target languages, which involved a shared attention mechanism strategy; Tu et al. (2016) proposed an attention coverage strategy, so that the model has explicit information from which source words are used to generate previous target words, and therefore addressed the problems of over- and under-translation.

Calixto et al. (2017b) has recently reported n-best list re-ranking experiments of e-commerce product listings using multi-modal eBay data. Whereas their focus is on improving translation quality with n-best list re-ranking experiments, in this work our focus is on the human evaluation of translations generated with the different text-only and multi-modal models. To the best of our knowledge, along with Calixto et al. (2017b) we are the first to study multi-modal NMT applied to the translation of product listings, i.e. for the e-commerce domain.

7 Conclusions and Future Work

In this paper, we investigate the potential impact of multi-modal NMT in the context of e-commerce product listings. Images bring important information to NMT models in this context; in fact, translations obtained with a multi-modal NMT model are preferred to ones obtained with a text-only model over 88% of the time. Nevertheless, humans still prefer phrase-based SMT over NMT output in this use-case. We attribute this to the nature of the task: listing titles have little syntactic structure and yet many rare words, which can produce many confusing neologisms especially if using subword units.

The core neural MT models still have to be improved significantly to address these challenges. However, in contrast to SMT, they already provide an effective way of improving MT quality with information contained in images. As future work, we will study the impact that additional back-translated data have on multi-modal NMT models.

Acknowledgements

The ADAPT Centre for Digital Content Technology (`www.adaptcentre.ie`) at Dublin City University is funded under the Science Foundation Ireland Research Centres Programme (Grant 13/RC/2106) and is co-funded under the European Regional Development Fund.

References

Dzmitry Bahdanau, Kyunghyun Cho, and Yoshua Bengio. 2015. Neural Machine Translation by Jointly Learning to Align and Translate. In *International Conference on Learning Representations. ICLR 2015*.

Yoshua Bengio, Réjean Ducharme, Pascal Vincent, and Christian Janvin. 2003. A Neural Probabilistic Language Model. *J. Mach. Learn. Res.*, 3:1137–1155.

Luisa Bentivogli, Arianna Bisazza, Mauro Cettolo, and Marcello Federico. 2016. Neural versus phrase-based machine translation quality: a case study. In *Proceedings of the 2016 Conference on Empirical Methods in Natural Language Processing*, pages 257–267, Austin, Texas, USA.

Ozan Caglayan, Walid Aransa, Yaxing Wang, Marc Masana, Mercedes García-Martínez, Fethi Bougares, Loïc Barrault, and Joost van de Weijer. 2016. Does multimodality help human and machine for translation and image captioning? In *Proceedings of the First Conference on Machine Translation*, pages 627–633, Berlin, Germany.

Iacer Calixto, Teofilo de Campos, and Lucia Specia. 2012. Images as context in Statistical Machine Translation. In *The 2nd Annual Meeting of the EPSRC Network on Vision & Language (VL'12)*, Sheffield, UK. EPSRC Vision and Language Network.

Iacer Calixto, Desmond Elliott, and Stella Frank. 2016. DCU-UvA Multimodal MT System Report. In *Proceedings of the First Conference on Machine Translation*, pages 634–638, Berlin, Germany.

Iacer Calixto, Qun Liu, and Nick Campbell. 2017a. Doubly-Attentive Decoder for Multi-modal Neural Machine Translation. *CoRR*, abs/1702.01287.

Iacer Calixto, Daniel Stein, Evgeny Matusov, Pintu Lohar, Sheila Castilho, and Andy Way. 2017b. Using images to improve machine-translating e-commerce product listings. In *Proceedings of the 15th Conference of the European Chapter of the Association for Computational Linguistics, EACL 2017*, Valencia, Spain (Paper Accepted).

Kyunghyun Cho, Bart van Merrienboer, Dzmitry Bahdanau, and Yoshua Bengio. 2014. On the Properties of Neural Machine Translation: Encoder-Decoder Approaches. In *Proceedings of SSST@EMNLP 2014, Eighth Workshop on Syntax, Semantics and Structure in Statistical Translation*, pages 103–111, Doha, Qatar.

Jonathan H. Clark, Chris Dyer, Alon Lavie, and Noah A. Smith. 2011. Better Hypothesis Testing for Statistical Machine Translation: Controlling for Optimizer Instability. In *Proceedings of the 49th Annual Meeting of the Association for Computational Linguistics: Human Language Technologies: Short Papers - Volume 2*, HLT '11, pages 176–181, Portland, Oregon.

Jacob Cohen. 1960. A Coefficient of Agreement for Nominal Scales. *Educational and Psychological Measurement*, 20(1):37–46.

Michael Denkowski and Alon Lavie. 2014. Meteor Universal: Language Specific Translation Evaluation for Any Target Language. In *Proceedings of the Ninth Workshop on Statistical Machine Translation*, pages 376–380, Baltimore, Maryland, USA.

Desmond Elliott, Stella Frank, Khalil Sima'an, and Lucia Specia. 2016. Multi30k: Multilingual english-german image descriptions. In *Workshop on Vision and Language at ACL '16*, Berlin, Germany.

Orhan Firat, Kyunghyun Cho, and Yoshua Bengio. 2016. Multi-Way, Multilingual Neural Machine Translation with a Shared Attention Mechanism. In *Proceedings of the 2016 Conference of the North American Chapter of the Association for Computational Linguistics: Human Language Technologies*, pages 866–875, San Diego, California.

Kaiming He, Xiangyu Zhang, Shaoqing Ren, and Jian Sun. 2016. Deep residual learning for image recognition. In *2016 IEEE Conference on Computer Vision and Pattern Recognition, CVPR 2016*, pages 770–778, Las Vegas, NV, USA.

Kenneth Heafield, Ivan Pouzyrevsky, Jonathan H. Clark, and Philipp Koehn. 2013. Scalable modified Kneser-Ney language model estimation. In *Proceedings of the 51st Annual Meeting of the Association for Computational Linguistics*, pages 690–696, Sofia, Bulgaria.

Julian Hitschler, Shigehiko Schamoni, and Stefan Riezler. 2016. Multimodal Pivots for Image Caption Translation. In *Proceedings of the 54th Annual Meeting of the Association for Computational Linguistics (Volume 1: Long Papers)*, pages 2399–2409, Berlin, Germany.

Po-Yao Huang, Frederick Liu, Sz-Rung Shiang, Jean Oh, and Chris Dyer. 2016. Attention-based Multimodal Neural Machine Translation. In *Proceedings of the First Conference on Machine Translation*, pages 639–645, Berlin, Germany.

Reinhard Kneser and Hermann Ney. 1995. Improved backing-off for m-gram language modeling. In *Proceedings of the IEEE International Conference on Acoustics, Speech and Signal Processing*, volume I, pages 181–184, Detroit, Michigan.

J. Richard Landis and Gary G. Koch. 1977. The measurement of observer agreement for categorical data. *Biometrics*, 33(1):159–174.

Jindřich Libovický, Jindřich Helcl, Marek Tlustý, Ondřej Bojar, and Pavel Pecina. 2016. CUNI System for WMT16 Automatic Post-Editing and Multimodal Translation Tasks. In *Proceedings of the First Conference on Machine Translation*, pages 646–654, Berlin, Germany.

Thang Luong, Hieu Pham, and Christopher D. Manning. 2015. Effective Approaches to Attention-based Neural Machine Translation. In *Proceedings of the 2015 Conference on Empirical Methods in Natural Language Processing (EMNLP)*, pages 1412–1421, Lisbon, Portugal.

Franz Josef Och. 2003. Minimum error rate training in statistical machine translation. In *Proceedings of the 41st Annual Meeting on Association for Computational Linguistics - Volume 1*, pages 160–167, Sapporo, Japan.

Kishore Papineni, Salim Roukos, Todd Ward, and Wei-Jing Zhu. 2002. Bleu: A method for automatic evaluation of machine translation. In *Proceedings of the 40th Annual Meeting on Association for Computational Linguistics*, ACL '02, pages 311–318, Philadelphia, Pennsylvania.

Maja Popović. 2015. chrF: character n-gram F-score for automatic MT evaluation. In *Proceedings of the Tenth Workshop on Statistical Machine Translation*, pages 392–395, Lisbon, Portugal.

Olga Russakovsky, Jia Deng, Hao Su, Jonathan Krause, Sanjeev Satheesh, Sean Ma, Zhiheng Huang, Andrej Karpathy, Aditya Khosla, Michael Bernstein, Alexander C. Berg, and Li Fei-Fei. 2015. ImageNet Large Scale Visual Recognition Challenge. *International Journal of Computer Vision (IJCV)*, 115(3):211–252.

Rico Sennrich, Barry Haddow, and Alexandra Birch. 2016. Neural machine translation of rare words with subword units. In *Proceedings of the 54th Annual Meeting of the Association for Computational Linguistics (Volume 1: Long Papers)*, pages 1715–1725, Berlin, Germany, August.

Kashif Shah, Josiah Wang, and Lucia Specia. 2016. SHEF-Multimodal: Grounding Machine Translation on Images. In *Proceedings of the First Conference on Machine Translation*, pages 660–665, Berlin, Germany.

Matthew Snover, Bonnie Dorr, Richard Schwartz, Linnea Micciulla, and John Makhoul. 2006. A study of translation edit rate with targeted human annotation. In *Proceedings of Association for Machine Translation in the Americas*, pages 223–231, Cambridge, MA, USA.

Lucia Specia, Stella Frank, Khalil Sima'an, and Desmond Elliott. 2016. A Shared Task on Multimodal Machine Translation and Crosslingual Image Description. In *Proceedings of the First Conference on Machine Translation, WMT 2016*, pages 543–553, Berlin, Germany.

Zhaopeng Tu, Zhengdong Lu, Yang Liu, Xiaohua Liu, and Hang Li. 2016. Modeling Coverage for Neural Machine Translation. In *Proceedings of the 54th Annual Meeting of the Association for Computational Linguistics (Volume 1: Long Papers)*, pages 76–85, Berlin, Germany.

Oriol Vinyals, Alexander Toshev, Samy Bengio, and Dumitru Erhan. 2015. Show and tell: A neural image caption generator. In *IEEE Conference on Computer Vision and Pattern Recognition, CVPR 2015*, pages 3156–3164, Boston, Massachusetts, USA.

Kelvin Xu, Jimmy Ba, Ryan Kiros, Kyunghyun Cho, Aaron Courville, Ruslan Salakhudinov, Rich Zemel, and Yoshua Bengio. 2015. Show, attend and tell: Neural image caption generation with visual attention. In *Proceedings of the 32nd International Conference on Machine Learning (ICML-15)*, pages 2048–2057, Lille, France.

Peter Young, Alice Lai, Micah Hodosh, and Julia Hockenmaier. 2014. From image descriptions to visual denotations: New similarity metrics for semantic inference over event descriptions. *Transactions of the Association for Computational Linguistics*, 2:67–78.

The BreakingNews Dataset

Arnau Ramisa*
Institut de Robòtica i Informàtica Industrial (CSIC-UPC), Barcelona, Spain
aramisa@iri.upc.edu

Fei Yan*
Centre for Vision, Speech and Signal Processing, University of Surrey, Guildford, UK
f.yan@surrey.ac.uk

Francesc Moreno-Noguer
Institut de Robòtica i Informàtica Industrial (CSIC-UPC), Barcelona, Spain
fmoreno@iri.upc.edu

Krystian Mikolajczyk
Department of Electrical and Electronic Engineering, Imperial College London, UK
k.mikolajczyk@imperial.ac.uk

Abstract

We present BreakingNews, a novel dataset with approximately 100K news articles including images, text and captions, and enriched with heterogeneous meta-data (e.g. GPS coordinates and popularity metrics). The tenuous connection between the images and text in news data is appropriate to take work at the intersection of Computer Vision and Natural Language Processing to the next step, hence we hope this dataset will help spur progress in the field.

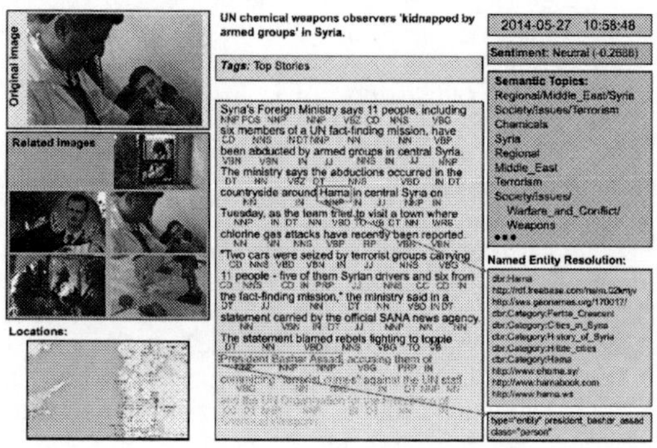

Figure 1: Example article with annotations from the BreakingNews dataset.

1 Introduction

Current successes in the crossroads between NLP and computer vision indicate that the techniques are mature for more challenging objectives than those posed by existing datasets. The NLP community has been addressing tasks such as sentiment analysis, popularity prediction, summarization, source identification or geolocation to name a few, that have been relatively little explored in computer vision. *BreakingNews* is a large-scale dataset[1] of news articles with rich meta-data and, we believe, an excellent benchmark for taking joint vision and language developments a step further. In contrast to existing datasets, the link between images and text in BreakingNews is not as direct, i.e., the objects, actions and attributes of the images may not explicitly appear as words in the text (see example in Fig. 1). The visual-language connections are more subtle and learning them will require the development of new inference tools able to reason at a higher and more abstract level. Furthermore, besides tackling article illustration or image captioning tasks, the proposed dataset is intended to address new challenges, such as source/media agency detection, estimation of GPS coordinates, or popularity prediction (which we annotate based on the reader comments and number of re-tweets).

In (Ramisa et al., 2016) we present several baseline results for different tasks using this dataset.

2 Description of the Dataset

The *BreakingNews* dataset consists of approximately 100,000 articles published between the 1st of January and the 31th of December of 2014. All articles include at least one image, and cover a wide variety of topics, including sports, politics, arts, healthcare or local news.

The main text of the articles was downloaded using the IJS newsfeed (Trampuš and Novak, 2012), which provides a clean stream of semantically enriched news articles in multiple languages from a pool of *rss* feeds.

We restricted the articles to those that were written in English, contained at least one image, and originated from a shortlist of highly-ranked news media agencies (see Table 1) to ensure a degree of

* denotes equal contribution

[1] http://www.iri.upc.edu/people/aramisa/BreakingNews/index.html

Proceedings of the 6th Workshop on Vision and Language, pages 38–39,
Valencia, Spain, April 4, 2017. ©2017 Association for Computational Linguistics

Source	num. articles	avg. len. article	avg. num. images	avg. len. caption	avg. num. comments	avg. len. comment	avg. num. shares	% geo-located
Yahoo News	10,834	521 ± 338	1.00 ± 0.00	40 ± 33	126 ± 658	39 ± 71	n/a	65.2%
BBC News	17,959	380 ± 240	1.54 ± 0.82	14 ± 4	7 ± 78	48 ± 21	n/a	48.7%
The Irish Independent	4,073	555 ± 396	1.00 ± 0.00	14 ± 14	1 ± 6	17 ± 5	4 ± 20	52.3%
Sydney Morning Herald	6,025	684 ± 395	1.38 ± 0.71	14 ± 10	6 ± 37	58 ± 55	718 ± 4976	60.4%
The Telegraph	29,757	700 ± 449	1.01 ± 0.12	16 ± 8	59 ± 251	45 ± 65	355 ± 2867	59.3%
The Guardian	20,141	786 ± 527	1.18 ± 0.59	20 ± 8	180 ± 359	53 ± 64	1509 ± 7555	61.5%
The Washington Post	9,839	777 ± 477	1.10 ± 0.43	25 ± 17	98 ± 342	43 ± 50	n/a	61.3%

Table 1: Dataset statistics. Mean and standard deviation, usually rounded to the nearest integer.

consistency and quality. Given the geographic distribution of the news agencies, most of the dataset is made of news stories in English-speaking countries in general, and the UK in particular. For each article we downloaded the images, image captions and user comments from the original article webpage. News article images are quite different from those in existing captioned images datasets like Flickr8K (Hodosh et al., 2013) or MS-COCO (Lin et al., 2014): often include close-up views of a person (46% of the pictures in BreakingNews contain faces) or complex scenes. Furthermore, news image captions use a much richer vocabulary than in existing datasets (e.g. Flickr8K has a total of 8,918 unique tokens, while eight thousand random captions from BreakingNews already have 28,028), and they rarely describe the exact contents of the picture.

We complemented the original article images with additional pictures downloaded from Google Images, using the full title of the article as search query. The five top ranked images of sufficient size in each search were downloaded as potentially related images (in fact, the original article image usually appears among them).

Regarding measures of article popularity, we downloaded all comments in the article page and the number of shares on different social networks (e.g. Twitter, Facebook, LinkedIn) if this information was available. Whenever possible, in addition to the full text of the comments, we recovered the thread structure, as well as the author, publication date, likes (and dislikes) and number of replies. Since there were no share or comments information available for "The Irish Independent", we searched Twitter using the full title and collected the tweets that mentioned a name associated with the newspaper (e.g. @Independent_ie, Irish Independent, @IndoBusiness) or with links to the original article in place of comments. We considered the collective number of re-tweets as shares of the article. The IJS Newsfeed annotates

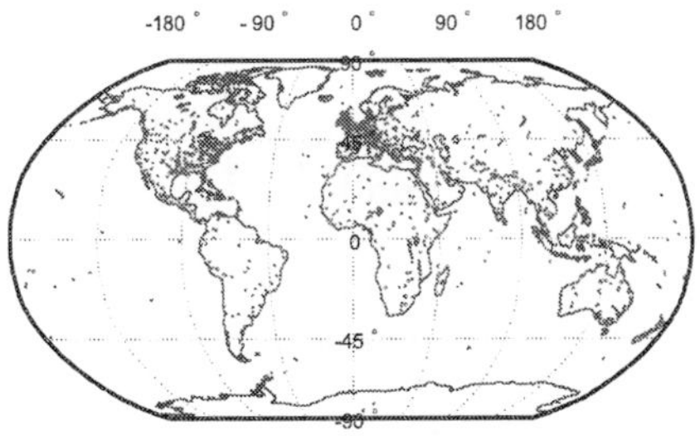

Figure 2: Ground truth geolocations of articles.

the articles with geolocation information both for the news agency and for the article content. This information is primarily taken from the provided RSS summary, but sometimes it is not available and then it is inferred from the article using heuristics such as the location of the publisher, TLD country, or the story text. Fig. 2 shows a distribution of news story geolocation.

Finally, the dataset is annotated for convenience with shallow and deep linguistic features (e.g. part of speech tags, inferred semantic topics, named entity detection and resolution, sentiment analysis) with *XLike* [2] and *Enrycher* [3] NLP pipelines.

References

M. Hodosh, P. Young, and J. Hockenmaier. 2013. Framing image description as a ranking task: Data, models and evaluation metrics. *Journal of Artificial Intelligence Research*, 47:853–899.

T. Lin, M. Maire, S. Belongie, J. Hays, P. Perona, D. Ramanan, P. Dollár, and C. Zitnick. 2014. Microsoft coco: Common objects in context. In *ECCV*, pages 740–755.

A. Ramisa, F. Yan, F. Moreno-Noguer, and K. Mikolajczyk. 2016. Breakingnews: Article annotation by image and text processing. *CoRR*, abs/1603.07141.

M. Trampuš and B. Novak. 2012. Internals of an aggregated web news feed. In *International Information Science Conference IS*, pages 431–434.

[2] `http://www.xlike.org/language-processing-pipeline/`

[3] `http://ailab.ijs.si/tools/enrycher/`

Automatic identification of head movements in video-recorded conversations: can words help?

Patrizia Paggio
University of Copenhagen
University of Malta
paggio@hum.ku.dk

Costanza Navarretta
University of Copenhagen
costanza@hum.ku.dk

Bart Jongejan
University of Copenhagen
bartj@hum.ku.dk

1 Introduction and background

Head movements are the most frequent gestures in face-to-face communication, and important for feedback giving (Allwood, 1988; Yngve, 1970; Duncan, 1972), and turn management (McClave, 2000).Their automatic recognition has been addressed by many multimodal communication researchers (Heylen et al., 2007; Paggio and Navarretta, 2011; Morency et al., 2007).

The method for automatic head movement annotation described in this paper is implemented as a plugin to the freely available multimodal annotation tool ANVIL (Kipp, 2004), using OpenCV (Bradski and Koehler, 2008), combined with a command line script that performs a number of file transformations and invokes the LibSVM software (Chang and Lin, 2011) to train and test a support vector classifier. Successively, the script produces a new annotation in ANVIL containing the learned head movements. The present method builds on (Jongejan, 2012) by adding jerk to the movement features and by applying machine learning. In this paper we also conduct a statistical analysis of the distribution of words in the annotated data to understand if word features could be used to improve the learning model.

Research aimed at the automatic recognition of head movements, especially nods and shakes, has addressed the issue in essentially two different ways. Thus a number of studies use data in which the face, or a part of it, has been tracked via various devices and typically train HMM models on such data (Kapoor and Picard, 2001; Tan and Rong, 2003; Wei et al., 2013). The accuracy reported i these studies is in the range 75-89%.

Other studies, on the contrary, try to identify head movements from raw video material using computer video techniques (Zhao et al., 2012; Morency et al., 2005). Different results are obtained depending on a number of factors such as video quality, lighting conditions, whether the movements are naturally occurring or rehearsed. The best results so far are probably those in (Morency et al., 2007), where an LDCRF model achieves an accuracy from 65% to 75% for a false positive rate of 20-30% and outperforms earlier SVM and HMM models.

Our work belongs to the latter strand of research in that we also work with raw video data.

2 Movement features

Three time-related derivatives with respect to the changing position of the face are used in this work as features for the identification of head movements: velocity, acceleration and jerk. Velocity is change of position per unit of time, acceleration is change of velocity per unit of time, and jerk is change of acceleration per unit of time. We expect that a sequence of frames for which jerk has a high value in the horizontal or vertical direction will correspond to the most effortful part of the head movement, often called *stroke* (Kendon, 2004).

3 Data, test setup, and results

The data come from the Danish NOMCO (Paggio et al., 2010), a video-recorded corpus of conversational interactions with many different annotation layers (Paggio and Navarretta, 2016), including type of head movement (nods, turns. etc).

For this work, two videos in which one of the participants is the same were selected at random, and only the head movements performed by this one participant are considered. One video is used for training, and the other for testing. In both videos, OpenCV is used to analyse each frame for the x and y coordinates of the participants's head, and based on these coordinates velocity, acceleration and jerk measures are calculated for each

Proceedings of the 6th Workshop on Vision and Language, pages 40–42,
Valencia, Spain, April 4, 2017. ©2017 Association for Computational Linguistics

Category	true	false
movement	29,980	11,960
non-movement	235,640	108,420
sum	265,620	120,380

Table 1: Distribution of true and false move and non-move sequences in milliseconds.

frame and added to the video annotation. In the video used for training, each frame is added a boolean feature indicating presence or absence of head movement in the manual annotation.

A first inspection of the classification results showed that in several cases the classifier detected sequences of movement interrupted by empty frames, where the manual annotation consisted of longer spans of uninterrupted movement. Therefore, empty spans (*margins*) of varying length were considered part of the movement annotation in the subsequent experiments, all performed with SVM. In all experiments, using all three movement features together yield the best results. When margin = 2 the ratio true positive/true negative is maximal. A maximum accuracy of 68%, however, is reached for a much higher value of the margin, 17 frames, or 0.68 seconds. For comparison, a baseline model always selecting non-movement would reach an accuracy of 64%. Counts for true and false movement and non-movement sequences detected by the classifier are shown in Table (1).

Even though we can do better than the baseline, the accuracy is still not adequate. Considering the fact that the annotators who created the gold standard had access to the audio channel when they identified the head movements, it is worth considering whether word features could be used to train more sophisticated and accurate models.

4 Head movements and words

The relation between head movements and words was investigated by looking at how different kinds of words are distributed over sequences of movement vs non-movements. We thus considered distributions where the word category includes only real words, also filled pauses, only filled pauses and feedback words, and finally only stressed words. In all cases, we are only looking at the speech stream of the person performing the movement. The last two distributions show the least interesting effects. Thus, feedback words have almost equal, and very low, probability to occur in movement and non-movement sequences. In the

	true	false
words	0.58	0.46
no words (incl. filled pauses)	0.42	0.54
words (incl. filled pauses)	0.75	0.73
no words	0.25	0.27
filled pauses and fb words	0.07	0.05
other words and no words	0.93	0.95
stressed words	0.31	0.25
unstressed words and no words	0.69	0.75

Table 2: Proportions of different word and no word categories in true and false movement sequences

	true	false
words	0.36	0.57
no words (incl. filled pauses)	0.64	0.43
words (incl. filled pauses)	0.56	0.76
no words	0.44	0.24
filled pauses and fb words	0.04	0.04
other words and no words	0.96	0.96
stressed words	0.20	0.28
unstressed words and no words	0.80	0.72

Table 3: Proportions of different word and no word categories in true and false non-movement sequences

case of stressed words, we see that their probability of occurring with movement is slightly higher than with non movement (31% vs 20%). If we look at the distribution of all words vs no words including filled pauses, we see that words have a 58% probability of occurring with movement, as opposed to a only 36% probability of occurring with non-movement. Finally, if we take words including filled pauses against no words, the probability of word occurrence with movement is 75% vs 56% with non-movement. Thus, distinguishing between real words and no words including filled pauses has the potential to differentiate best between presence and absence of movement in that we see that in this case the mutual proportion between word and no words goes in opposite directions depending on the sequence type. The differences in the distribution in this case are significant on a chi-square test in both movement and non-movement sequences. All the probabilities are summed up in Tables (2) and (3) .

To conclude, we have presented an approach where an SVM classifier is trained to recognise movement sequences based on velocity, acceleration, and jerk. A preliminary investigation of the overlap between temporal sequences classified as either movement or non-movement and the speech stream of the person performing the gesture shows that using word features may help increase the accuracy of the model, which is now 68%.

References

Sames Al Moubayed, Malek Baklouti, Mohamed Chetouani, Thierry Dutoit, Ammar Mahdhaoui, J-C Martin, Stanislav Ondas, Catherine Pelachaud, Jérôme Urbain, and Mehmet Yilmaz. 2009. Generating robot/agent backchannels during a storytelling experiment. In *Robotics and Automation, 2009. ICRA'09. IEEE International Conference on*, pages 3749–3754. IEEE.

Jens Allwood, Loredana Cerrato, Kristiina Jokinen, Costanza Navarretta, and Patrizia Paggio. 2007. The MUMIN Coding Scheme for the Annotation of Feedback, Turn Management and Sequencing. *Multimodal Corpora for Modelling Human Multimodal Behaviour. Special Issue of the International Journal of Language Resources and Evaluation*, 41(3–4):273–287.

Jens Allwood. 1988. The Structure of Dialog. In Martin M. Taylor, Franoise Neél, and Don G. Bouwhuis, editors, *Structure of Multimodal Dialog II*, pages 3–24. John Benjamins, Amsterdam.

G. Bradski and A. Koehler. 2008. *Learning OpenCV: Computer Vision with the OpenCV Linbrary*. O'Reilly.

Chih-Chung Chang and Chih-Jen Lin. 2011. Libsvm: A library for support vector machines. In *ACM Transactions on Intelligent Systems and Technology*.

Starkey Duncan. 1972. Some signals and rules for taking speaking turns in conversations. *Journal of Personality and Social Psychology*, 23:283–292.

D. Heylen, E. Bevacqua, M. Tellier, and C. Pelachaud. 2007. Searching for prototypical facial feedback signals. In *Proceedings of 7th International Conference on Intelligent Virtual Agents*, pages 147–153.

Kristiina Jokinen and Graham Wilcock. 2014. Automatic and manual annotations in first encounter dialogues. In *Human Language Technologies - The Baltic Perspective: Proceedings of the 6th International Conference Baltic HLT 2014*, volume 268 of *Frontiers in Artificial Intelligence and Applications*, pages 175–178.

Bart Jongejan, 2012. *Automatic annotation of head velocity and acceleration in Anvil*, pages 201–208. European language resources distribution agency, 5.

Ashish Kapoor and Rosalind W. Picard. 2001. A real-time head nod and shake detector. In *Proceedings of the 2001 Workshop on Perceptive User Interfaces*, PUI '01, pages 1–5, New York, NY, USA. ACM.

Adam Kendon. 2004. *Gesture*. Cambridge University Press.

Michael Kipp. 2004. *Gesture Generation by Imitation – From Human Behavior to Computer Character Animation*. Boca Raton, Florida: Dissertation.com.

Evelyn McClave. 2000. Linguistic functions of head movements in the context of speech. *Journal of Pragmatics*, 32:855–878.

L.-P. Morency, C. Sidner, C. Lee, and T. Darrell. 2005. Contextual recognition of head gestures. In *Proc. Int. Conf. on Multimodal Interfaces (ICMI)*.

Louis-Philippe Morency, Ariadna Quattoni, and Trevor Darrell. 2007. Latent-dynamic discriminative models for continuous gesture recognition. In *2007 IEEE conference on computer vision and pattern recognition*, pages 1–8. IEEE.

P. Paggio and C. Navarretta. 2011. Head movements, facial expressions and feedback in danish first encounters interactions: A culture-specific analysis. In Constantine Stephanidis, editor, *Universal Access in Human-Computer Interaction- Users Diversity. 6th International Conference. UAHCI 2011, Held as Part of HCI International 2011*, number 6766 in LNCS, pages 583–690, Orlando Florida. Springer Verlag.

P. Paggio and C. Navarretta. 2016. The Danish NOMCO corpus multimodal interaction in first acquaintance conversations. *International Journal of Language Resources and Evaluation*, pages 1–32.

P. Paggio, J. Allwood, E. Ahlsén, K. Jokinen, and C. Navarretta. 2010. The NOMCO multimodal Nordic resource - goals and characteristics. In *Proceedings of the Seventh conference on International Language Resources and Evaluation (LREC'10)*.

W. Tan and G. Rong. 2003. A real-time head nod and shake detector using hmms. *Expert Systems with Applications*, 25(3):461–466.

Haolin Wei, Patricia Scanlon, Yingbo Li, David S Monaghan, and Noel E O'Connor. 2013. Real-time head nod and shake detection for continuous human affect recognition. In *2013 14th International Workshop on Image Analysis for Multimedia Interactive Services (WIAMIS)*, pages 1–4. IEEE.

Victor Yngve. 1970. On getting a word in edgewise. In *Papers from the sixth regional meeting of the Chicago Linguistic Society*, pages 567–578.

Z. Zhao, Y. Wang, and S. Fu. 2012. Head movement recognition based on lucas-kanade algorithm. In *Computer Science Service System (CSSS), 2012 International Conference on*, pages 2303–2306, Aug.

Multi-Modal Fashion Product Retrieval

A. Rubio
Institut de Robòtica i Informàtica Industrial (CSIC-UPC)
Wide Eyes Technologies
arubio@iri.upc.edu

LongLong Yu
Wide Eyes Technologies
longyu@wide-eyes.it

E. Simo-Serra
Waseda University
esimo@aoni.waseda.jp

F. Moreno-Noguer
Institut de Robòtica i Informàtica Industrial (CSIC-UPC)
fmoreno@iri.upc.edu

Abstract

Finding a product in the fashion world can be a daunting task. Everyday, e-commerce sites are updating with thousands of images and their associated metadata (textual information), deepening the problem. In this paper, we leverage both the images and textual metadata and propose a joint multi-modal embedding that maps both the text and images into a common latent space. Distances in the latent space correspond to similarity between products, allowing us to effectively perform retrieval in this latent space. We compare against existing approaches and show significant improvements in retrieval tasks on a large-scale e-commerce dataset.

1 Introduction

The level of traffic of modern e-commerce is growing fast. U.S. retail e-commerce, for instance, was expected to grow 16.6% on 2016 Christmas holidays (after a 15.3% increase in 2014) (Walton, 2016). In order to adapt to these trend, sellers must provide a good experience with easy to find and well classified products. In this work, we consider the problem of multi-modal retrieval, in which a user searches for either text or images given a text or image query. Existing approaches for retrieval focus image-only and require hard to obtain datasets for training (Hadi Kiapour et al., 2015). Instead, we opt to leverage easily obtained metadata for training our model, and learning a mapping from text and images to a common latent space, in which distances correspond to similarity.

We evaluate our approach in the retrieval and classification tasks and it outperforms KCCA (Bach and Jordan, 2002) and Bag-of-word features on a large e-commerce dataset.

Text query:

ELEVENTY, piquet, solid color, polo collar, long sleeves, no appliqués, no pockets, small sized. 100% Cotton.

Closest images:

Figure 1: Example of a text and nearest images from the test set. Our embedding produces low distances between texts and images referring to similar objects.

2 Method

Our joint multi-modal embedding approach consists of a neural network with two branches: one for image and one for text. The image branch is based on the Alexnet (Krizhevsky et al., 2012) Convolutional Neural Network (CNN) which converts a 227×227 pixel image into a fixed-size 128-dimensional vector. The text branch is based on a multi-layer neural network and uses as an input features extracted by a pre-trained *word2vec* network which are converted into a fixed-size 128-dimensional vector. Both branches are trained jointly such that the 128-dimensional output space becomes a joint embedding by minimizing the distance between related image-text pairs and maximizing the distance between unrelated image-text pairs using the contrastive loss function (Hadsell et al., 2006) shown in 1, where v_I and v_T are two embedded vectors corresponding to the image and the text respectively, y is a label that indicates whether or not the two vectors are compatible ($y = 0$) or dissimilar ($y = 1$), and m is a margin for the negatives. Two auxiliary classification

Proceedings of the 6th Workshop on Vision and Language, pages 43–45,
Valencia, Spain, April 4, 2017.

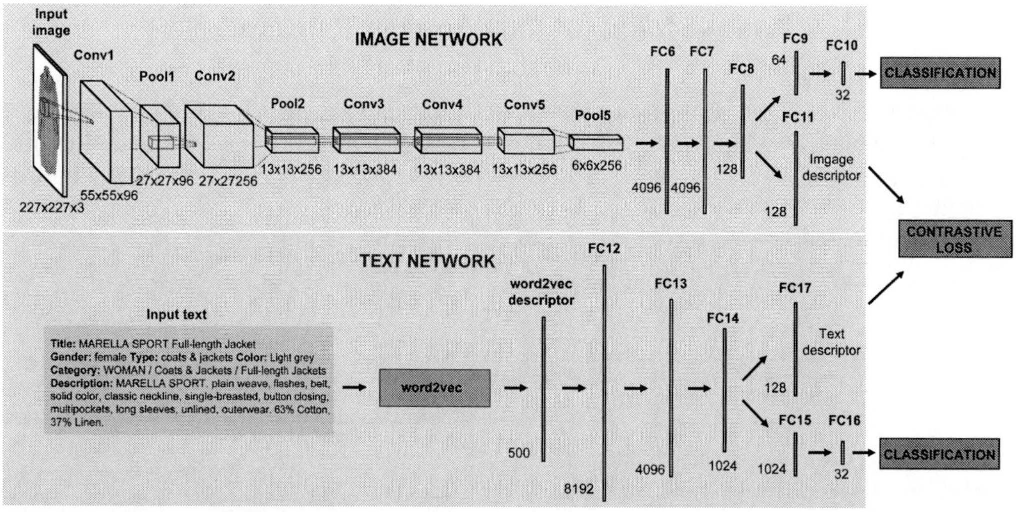

Figure 2: Architecture of the neural network used. *Conv*, *Pool* and *FC* refer to convolutional, pooling and fully connected layers, respectively. When sizes of two dimensions are equal, some of them are omitted for clarity. Fully connected layers are uni-dimensional. *Text descriptor* and *Image descriptor* are the embedded vectors describing the input text and image, respectively.

Table 1: Results of our method compared to *KCCA* and our method using *Bag of Words* for text representation.

Model	Median rank	
	Img v. txt	**Txt v. img**
KCCA	52.42%	46.65%
Bag of Words	4.50%	4.54%
word2vec	1.61%	1.63%

networks are also used during training that encourages the joint embedding to also encode semantic concepts. An overview can be seen in Fig. 2.

$$L_C(v_I, v_T, y) = (1-y)\frac{1}{2}\left(\|v_I - v_T\|_2\right)^2 + (y)\frac{1}{2}\left\{\max\left(0, m - \|v_I - v_T\|_2\right)\right\}^2 \tag{1}$$

3 Results

Next, we describe the results obtained by applying our method to a Fashion e-commerce dataset of $431,841$ images of fashion products with associated texts, classified in 32 categories (such as *boots*, *jewelry*, *skirt*, *shirt*, *dress*, *backpack*, *swimwear*, *glasses/sunglasses*, *shorts*, *sandals*, etc.). In order to evaluate our method, we compute all the 128-dimensional descriptors of images and texts in the testing set. Then, use the text as queries to obtain the images, and vice-versa. Looking at the position at which the exact match is, we compute the median rank for each case. The resultant values are below 2%, meaning that the exact match is usually closer than the 98% of the dataset, beating the result obtained by KCCA[1] and by our same architecture substituting the *word2vec* by a classical *Bag of Words*. We compare this metrics with two baselines: a version of our method replacing *word2vec* by *Bag of Words* and KCCA (see Table 1. We also obtained a recall value of nearly 80% for the top 5%, meaning that 80% of times the exact match for the input query is in the closest 5% results. At the same time, for the classification task we obtain accuracy values of 90% for images and 99% for texts with the *word2vec* approach.

4 Conclusions

We have presented an approach for joint multimodal embedding with neural networks with a focus on the fashion domain that is easily amenable to large existing e-commerce datasets by exploiting readily available images and their associated metadata, and can be easily used for retrieval tasks.

[1]The KCCA model has been trained with less descriptors (only 10000) due to memory errors when trying to use the whole training set

References

F. R. Bach and M. I. Jordan. 2002. Kernel independent component analysis. *JMLR*, 3(Jul):1–48.

M. Hadi Kiapour, X. Han, S. Lazebnik, Alexander C. Berg, and Tamara L. Berg. 2015. Where to buy it: Matching street clothing photos in online shops. In *CVPR*.

Raia Hadsell, Sumit Chopra, and Yann LeCun. 2006. Dimensionality reduction by learning an invariant mapping. In *CVPR*.

A. Krizhevsky, I. Sutskever, and G. E. Hinton. 2012. Imagenet classification with deep convolutional neural networks. In *NIPS*.

D. Walton. 2016. *The Ultimate List of E-Commerce Stats for Holiday 2016*. `http://blog.marketingadept.com/the-ultimate-list-of-e-commerce-marketing-stats-for-holiday-2016/`. Accessed: 2017-01-23.

Author Index

Birmingham, Brandon, 11

Calixto, Iacer, 31
Castilho, Sheila, 31

Eshghi, Arash, 1

Jongejan, Bart, 40

Lemon, Oliver, 1

Matusov, Evgeny, 31
Mikolajczyk, Krystian, 38
Mills, Gregory, 1
Moens, Marie-Francine, 21
Moreno-Noguer, Francesc, 38, 43
Muscat, Adrian, 11

Navarretta, Costanza, 40
Nurani Venkitasubramanian, Aparna, 21

Paggio, Patrizia, 40

Ramisa, Arnau, 38
Rubio Romano, Antonio, 43

Simo-Serra, Edgar, 43
Stein, Daniel, 31

Tuytelaars, Tinne, 21

Way, Andy, 31

Yan, Fei, 38
Yu, LongLong, 43
Yu, Yanchao, 1

Association for Computational Linguistics
209 N. Eighth Street
Stroudsburg, Pennsylvania 18360

ISBN 978-1-5108-3873-4

CURRAN ASSOCIATES INC.
proceedings.com